"I'd recommend this book to seminary formators and direc-
~~~~~ of houses of formation. It is a book they should read."

Fr Miguel Garaizabal, SJ

lissionary for 53 years in Thailand and
: spiritual director for the last 30 years

"The explanations and presentations are very clear and read-
er-friendly. I like the case studies that were included... they
give the reader a feel of the underlying dynamics that could
contribute to the development of same-sex attractions. The
book is an eye-opener to the fact that same-sex attractions
are a symptom of problems in the family and society; giving
a challenge for people to take action to face these problems."

Jane Lee

Counsellor-administrator at Door of Hope Counseling Resource Center,
Philippines for 21 years; trained in Psychology, Christian Counseling and
Christian Spiritual Direction; board member of the Philippine Associa-
tion of Christian Counselors and Asian Christian Counselors Association

"Based on the experience of my own life, in addition to what
I have learned from others about commonly held beliefs/nar-
ratives on the LGBTQ topic, I think this book is a 'must-read'.
It provides an understanding that is rare and often missing
from the greater picture. I sincerely hope that people near
and far will open their hearts and minds to what this great
resource has to offer."

Andrew

Former LGBTQ, now also a committed Christian, Canada

"As a parent, after searching for answers and ways to understand our son better, this book was such a blessing. It is easy to read, full of wisdom, well-researched, clear, compassionate and incredibly insightful. I felt for the first time a sense of peace and encouragement on our journey as parents. An important read for all parents."

Homemaker

Married and mother of three children, Australia

"Shen's motivation is to reduce misunderstanding in conservative religious communities that often condemn people with same-sex attractions. He emphasises that these are not chosen, but result from a number of contributing factors beyond the control of individuals. His goal is to educate families and communities to eliminate condemnation and rejection of these individuals, and instead to be empowered to relate with understanding and compassion. None of the information goes against the teachings of the Church."

Rev Esther Wakeman, Ph.D.

Lecturer, McGilvary College of Divinity, Payap University

The Un-affirmed Core

Understanding the Factors Behind
and Around Homosexuality

SECOND EDITION

Bryan Shen

Marshall Cavendish Editions

First published in 2018 by Armour Publishing

This Second Edition published in 2022 by Marshall Cavendish Editions
An imprint of Marshall Cavendish International

A member of the
Times Publishing Group

Other Marshall Cavendish Offices:
Marshall Cavendish Corporation, 800 Westchester Ave, Suite N-641, Rye Brook,
NY 10573, USA • Marshall Cavendish International (Thailand) Co Ltd, 253 Asoke,
16th Floor, Sukhumvit 21 Road, Klongtoey Nua, Wattana, Bangkok 10110, Thailand
• Marshall Cavendish (Malaysia) Sdn Bhd, Times Subang, Lot 46, Subang Hi-Tech
Industrial Park, Batu Tiga, 40000 Shah Alam, Selangor Darul Ehsan, Malaysia

Marshall Cavendish is a registered trademark of Times Publishing Limited

National Library Board, Singapore Cataloguing-in-Publication Data

Name(s): Shen, Bryan, 1960-
Title: The un-affirmed core : understanding the factors behind and around
homosexuality / Bryan Shen.
Other Title(s): Understanding the factors behind and around homosexuality
Description: Second edition. | Singapore : Marshall Cavendish Editions, 2022. |
First published in 2018 by Armour Publishing.
Identifier(s): ISBN 978-981-5066-96-8 (paperback)
Subject(s): LCSH: Homosexuality. | Homosexuality--Psychological aspects. |
Gender identity.
Classification: DDC 306.766--dc23

Printed in Singapore

Contents

Acknowledgements

I would like to thank the many friends from various walks of life and disciplines who have provided helpful comments and feedback. They include heads of professional bodies, religious leaders, priests and many extraordinary people. Prayers and support from them and many others are also much appreciated.

I would also like to thank Christina Lim and Armour Publishing for helping to get this book project off the ground.

And last but not least, to my mother for her constant faith.

Dedication

This book is dedicated to my many clients who have shared their deepest stories while also doing their utmost best in their lives including the social, religious and spiritual aspects. It is even more heroic when we consider their strife despite the lonely silence in the depths of their souls... sometimes feeling a constant threat of shame and derision, and carrying an enormous sense of incongruence. While the rest of the world tries to remember that "to err is human, to forgive is divine", they have a guillotine consciousness that "to err is unforgivable". And so they strive for perfection, oftentimes to the limits of their physical, mental and spiritual strength, and sometimes beyond.

This book is for all social, cultural, political and religious leaders of the world. Because, among the very best of people serving them are the very same people this book is dedicated to. It is my deepest wish that this book sparks a social transformation that enables these people to rise up and tackle head-on the greater issues surrounding gender identity development. Because the stones that are rejected can become the cornerstones of stronger houses.

Note

For all case stories in this book, names and identifiers have been changed or omitted to protect identities while keeping the substance of the case intact. The stories are placed where a precept explained could be seen in a real case. Most cases are complex and other factors may be involved. Therefore, some cross-referencing to other chapters may be required. Importantly, please respect the confidentiality of the people in these stories and pay due honour by not endeavouring to identify or disclose who they are.

Foreword

Homosexuality is a polarising and sensitive topic, more so now than ever before. This is especially so in communities where conservative-religious as well as liberal attitudes are increasing among social media users. What is needed is a body of information that attempts to bridge the wide divide.

In proportion to the divide, any information has to be comprehensive. What makes it more challenging is that much of our behaviour is driven by what is below our consciousness. And what is not conscious has no words or description. Neither then would any awareness of psychological cause and effect exist.

Therein lies the importance of psychology and research to help elucidate, differentiate and explain what would otherwise be an unintentional use of conflated words and simplified notions that only escalate social contentions.

Yet today, so many segments of society weigh in with what (little) they know. Understandably, each feels compelled to do so because they feel so much is at stake. On one hand, lives are at risk of suicides, depression and other mental health issues with continued misconceptions and negative regard. On the other hand, centuries of civil culture and religion that guided humanity to distinguish itself from base behaviours are at risk of being weakened and diminished. Unknown for so long are neglected issues in the family and society that deepened these problems in complex ways.

Until now, a systemic way to understand the sex scandals that rock some religious institutions has been elusive. To that end, this book seeks to provide a psychological and qualitative view in explaining why some religious leaders, who are supposed to be the most trusted people to guide religious communities, may also have the propensity to violate minors sexually.

This book should be read as a bridge between the multiple interpretations and positions on this topic. Some of the bridging frameworks (in Chapter 4) that Bryan introduces in this book might be new to some. I invite further investigation and explorations of such a discovery!

I have known Bryan for several years as a clinical member of the Singapore Association for Counselling, as a fellow counselling professional, clinical supervisor, and trainer. Bryan has constantly demonstrated the pursuit of the refinement of well-established precepts of the psychological sciences, and evidence to support his practice. This book is a clear demonstration that Bryan stands on continuing psychological research on gender identity and role development, real-life cases through his client work, the complex socialisation and family processes, and the resultant outcome of such experiences. He is able to present his findings clearly in an honest, factual, non-prescriptive, and non-judgemental way.

Whether you are a counselling professional, a pastor or a religious leader, a religious follower or a free thinker, a parent or a curious reader, heterosexual or homosexual… I pray your endeavours for the Truth be fruitful. May you have the courage, love and compassion to resolve the long-standing systemic problems and go on to help individuals, families and society. May you be able to do what it takes to bring forth understanding, unity, and peace from the divide.

Sam Kuna

President

Singapore Association for Counselling

Preface

I became a missionary in 1997 and soon based myself in Indo-China. As I became more fluent in the local language, I noticed that the locals would tell me deeply personal matters they would not tell anyone in their society. I decided to take up studies in Counselling and soon found myself the only qualified professional counsellor who could speak the local language. Very quickly, I was asked to help the young men in religious training houses. They would tell me deep secrets they did not tell anyone. That was how I started listening and helping many good and upright young men struggling with homosexuality. And I learnt much from them. I realised that educating the people around them that mattered was very important. I started giving talks to conservative-religious communities. These talks were hugely appreciated, not only because the information filled an important need to understand, but also because it helped to reduce social misconceptions, prejudice, ignorance-based fears and fear-based attitudes. I was asked to speak to many communities in Asia, and even to others beyond. "Your talk was too short", "we need more information", and "we need more speakers like you" were (and still are) some common feedback I received. That was how the need for this book arose.

However, writing in English for readers from different

parts of the world was not easy. Indeed, there are many differences in the way English words are used and understood in different parts of the world, especially when English isn't a reader's main cultural language. The different levels of sensitivities surrounding the subject of homosexuality in different societies heightened the challenge. Yet, the heartfelt stories shared with me, and the insights I have gained, pushed me to not leave this information unknown.

When this book was first published in 2018, its main objective was to educate conservative-religious communities to avoid judging children as "wrong", especially by people most important to them; to provide convincing information that the experience of same-sex attraction is not something one chooses, and to make clear what is harmful. To that end, this book has been successful. But I hope you can also understand its limitations. The concerns and interest of people in conservative-religious communities are rarely similar to the concerns and interests of people in liberal societies.

This second edition maintains its main objective, but it also includes information that would hopefully spur more research on developmental issues in the field of psychology and social neuroscience. I have tried to cater to the sensitivities of as many cultures as possible, and in so doing, I had a lot of limitations to work within. However, I am thankful to many people, from the far corners of the world, who have given me their feedback and assistance. May the benefits of this book reach those who need it, to the furthest ends of the earth.

Message

Bryan Shen approaches the difficult subject of homosexuality with wisdom and experience. Having served as a professional counsellor in four different Asian nations, he has ministered insight and strength to many people, and thought carefully about their experiences. *The Un-Affirmed Core* gives a fresh, careful, and compassionate look at the great diversity and commonalities among people who grow up in traditional cultures and have same-sex attractions. Shen's basic approach to the topic seeks to cut through cultural and political ambiguities to the psychological formation of the homosexual experience. The following are some of the major ideas I have seen at play in his writing:

- Exclusive romantic or sexual attraction to members of one's own sex is a real experience that many people have. Speaking in broad terms, it is not chosen, and it is not imaginary.
- Homosexual orientation arises from a complex but recognisable set of internal and environmental factors that form one's psyche during childhood. Especially in traditional societies, a man or woman with same-sex attractions may take many years or

even decades after puberty to begin to recognise his or her same-sex attractions, but this process of discovery also follows recognisable patterns.

- Once formed, sexual orientation is generally not reversible. However, same-sex attractions need not be expressed in the standard and often ambiguous forms of the current Western LGBT+ movement. That is to say that the true patterns and needs of same-sex attractions are not always the ones that are claimed by identifying oneself as "gay".

- Men and women with same-sex attractions are often highly spiritual by nature, as well as unusually gifted and motivated in other ways. They have an enormous amount to offer to their religious, civic, and familial communities. They also have special vulnerabilities that should be learnt with respect.

- Because world cultures are just beginning to understand homosexuality (both conservative cultures that have hardly acknowledged it at all, and progressive cultures that have taken an "anything goes" approach), we are in a unique time when the earnest study and care we give to people with same-sex attractions have an enormous power to help them, and their future successors, to find better roles in our communities than was ever possible before.

The case studies that Shen relays to illustrate his psychological observations are a special highlight of the book. For those many readers who have heard the intimate life stories of at most one or two friends with same-sex attractions, this book's case stories, which are based on real lives, will offer a wealth of new material for reflection. Furthermore, in light of Shen's thesis that homosexuality emerges in relation to one's own specific experience of family dynamics, gender roles, and educational environment, the fact that Shen's case studies are from non-Western cultures is a significant merit. While the dynamics described are universal, stories from the context of more tradition-based Asian families make his writing in many cases more relevant to a worldwide audience than that of authors who know only Western ways of growing up.

Another special strength of the book is the way it facilitates rich, thoughtful connections between modern psychology and a traditional sexual ethic. Shen's chapter on how a person with same-sex attractions becomes aware of his or her condition over time is an excellent example, as is his treatment of the possibilities of gas-lighting and sexual abuse within organisations.

This book should be a precious source of enlightenment and insight for people in conservative-religious communities who are ready to begin thinking about people with same-sex attractions in a serious way.

Rev (Dr) Fr Joseph Van House, OCist.

Fr Van House is a Cistercian monk at the Abbey of Our Lady of Dallas that runs a Preparatory School for boys. He was a Chaplain for "Courage" which ministers to individuals with unwanted same-sex attractions. He holds a Licentiate in Sacred Theology from the Pontifical Gregorian University in Rome. He obtained his Doctorate in Historical and Dogmatic Theology from Catholic University of America in 2020.

Introduction

For too long, the issue of homosexuality has been condemned or avoided on one hand and experienced in silent anguish or struggle-for-survival on the other. Prejudice and fear still exist. Ignorance is widespread while shallow acceptance is also spreading rapidly.

Maintaining the controversy is the nature of psychology, where much of what is happening occurs below consciousness. What is not conscious often has no proper words to describe, or at best is vague, nebulous, polysemous and cannot be understood, either distinctively or as a part of a bio-psychological system that can have a social function. Most people in everyday life do not walk around with an awareness of how their own biological psychology, environmental psychology, individual phenomenology, polyvagal system, attachment style and cognitive dissonance are influencing their perceptions, inclinations and actions. How can they then be aware of how these are working in others?

With these in mind, this book is written for leaders of conservative-religious societies and communities. Included are parents, teachers, relatives and anyone with a personal interest to know the depth and breadth of issues surrounding sexuality. While this book attempts to meet their interests and needs, it is by no means complete—for it is important to acknowledge the greater knowledge that has still yet to be found.

Allow me to illustrate with the analogy of leprosy. For many centuries, all holy books required lepers to live apart; whereby no contact with the population was allowed, their clothes had to be burnt, etc. Yet, it was still possible to have a pastoral ministry to lepers, which required courage and the removal of fears and prejudices. Such ministry might be similar to palliative care. Personal stories of human struggles can convert a fearful prejudiced heart towards openness and a caring disposition. The bacterium that causes leprosy was discovered in 1873. It took almost another century before the drugs that could treat leprosy became widely available. Today, if a religious person were to say, "My holy book has the final word. I don't need to know what science tells us about leprosy", then that religious person would be in grave error. Also, if people in the ministry that helped lepers were to say, "Our work has been going on for centuries. We know what to do, and we don't need to know what science tells us about leprosy", then these people would also be wrong to limit themselves to what they know. They would be depriving the people they serve of something additionally beneficial. So we must always be open to consider new information that builds up, corrects or refines the truth. If both these groups were to consider what science knows, to update and/or to refine their religious or pastoral views, I believe it would be possible to reduce divides, polarisations and misconceptions.

The aim of this book is to provide information—using precepts and views from the psychological sciences—to reduce prejudice, misinformation, fear and misunderstanding. There are many contributing factors interacting in complex ways which this book tries to identify and explain so that future research may be better designed and directed.

This book explains why a person who experiences same-sex attractions does not choose to have them, despite the fact that a "gay gene" has not been found. (The largest study to date was recently published in *Science Journal*. It involved genomes of nearly half a million people. The lead study author, Andre Ganna, a geneticist, concluded that "There is no 'gay gene'". See Note 1 on page 127 for more details.) This book goes further to explain how it is possible to have homosexuality without any discernible family dysfunction or external abuse whatsoever, and so to show that even praiseworthy families, religious or otherwise, are not exempt from these experiences being a reality among their family members. There are also explanations as to why people who experience same-sex attractions are often very talented, perfectionists, high-achievers and people who desire greatly to be role models.

Nonetheless, I hope this book can still be useful for those who strive to serve the LGBTQ+ community. The information it contains can help to reduce suicides, ostracisation, misconception and the constant fear of denigration. This book acknowledges the myriad of problems they face as it seeks to identify deep core issues and to help find ways to reduce the stress, both conscious and unconscious, that frequently assails them, thus compelling the need for relief.

While there are many books with the same aim written from the "spiritual-pastoral" (i.e. religious or theological) perspective, there are few books written from the view of the psychological sciences. However, I want to stress that the most effective way to help people struggling with homosexuality is *to include both the "spiritual-pastoral" approach as well as the psychological-assistive approach*. One without the other is only half as good.

And there is an additional problem about "half as good". Allow me to explain by first using what Victor E. Frankl (author of *Man's Search for Meaning*) wrote:

> … a man's suffering is similar to the behaviour of a gas. If a certain quantity of gas is pumped into an empty chamber, it will fill the chamber completely and evenly… Thus suffering completely fills the human soul and conscious mind, no matter whether the suffering is great or little.

Conversely, what happens when suffering is reduced is similar. If a part of the gas is removed, the relief is also felt completely and evenly. The person may say, "Ok, I'm fine, I can manage on my own now." This is the reason why many people don't finish their medication. It's more likely to happen if there is a need to show that he/she is able, capable, healthy, of little trouble, etc. Among people who experience same-sex attractions, this need is stronger (reasons are explained in Chapter 4). When they find relief of some kind, for example, finding acceptance in any community, the relief they experience is "good enough". They do not strive to discover the factors in their lives that may be contributing to the existence of these attractions.

As such, I find it is important to give an understanding of homosexuality in as complete a manner as possible in any educational endeavour. A more complete awareness can lead to a more comprehensive range of measures to help people navigate and respond to the existence of those attractions, especially when they (those attractions/inclinations) are very much unwanted. I find it terribly sad that many people today can only take in "sound bites" due to busyness and preoccupation. And they seem happy to have a little understanding even though there can be more. I think it is terrible when people in authority say, "Tell me in a few sentences what homosexuality is all about, because that's all the time I can afford." And it's worse when they fear to hear the truth because they have taken a stand and do not want to lose face.

In Epistemology—which is about the nature of knowledge—some philosophers maintain that there should be important distinctions between:

1. "Knowing that" (Knowledge via perception)
2. "Knowing how" (Knowledge of operation)
3. "Knowing by being in a community" (Knowledge via acquaintance)

People who experience same-sex attractions "know that" it is not chosen; it just is, and to them, it feels as in-born as can be. And there are also many people who have acquired "knowledge by being acquainted" with their friends who identify as LGBTQ+, or on the other hand are part of a conservative-religious community, culture or society that hold beliefs that are not affirmative of LGBTQ+ ideologies and perhaps are sometimes even seen as "homophobic". What is lacking is "knowing how" same-sex attractions can develop below consciousness in some family dynamics. However, there are at present two forces that suppress this knowledge. The first is by activists to remove any source of knowledge that explains the "how". Reasons include the fear that it would give rise to a "gay cure". In early July 2019, Amazon banned the sale of about 20 books of such nature, which were branded by activists as "gay cure" books. But this fear of "knowing how" negates many benefits; from cultivating better strategies to cope with anxiety, Obsessive-Compulsive Disorder (OCD), depression, loneliness, intimate partner violence and suicides, to the reduction of prejudice, rejection, denigration, sham marriages and abuses in conservative-religious communities. The second, which is even more lamentable, is a wilful avoidance of wanting to "know how" by leaders of some conservative-religious communities. I can only guess that it comes from the fear of not wanting to spark controversy and a lack of courage to deal with problems with knowledge, understanding, counsel and wisdom.

I must add a few words of caution to parents. You might feel pangs of guilt and regret when you are reading certain parts of this book. You might feel it even if your children have turned out fine. If they did—and many do despite parental deficiencies, whether they realise it or not—they are a testament to two things. The first is that children and parents have the ability to correct themselves along the way. And secondly, being part of a community that practises their faith in a good way is beneficial and important. However, for parents whose children did not, the feelings of guilt and regret can be very heavy. Do not be hard on yourselves as there are many unknown factors when one is raising a child and every child is different in temperament. These impact their relationships and play some role in the formation of their expectations, and how they think they ought to respond to circumstances in life in any context. I sincerely hope this book will help to fill important gaps. A religious community that practises compassion, mercy, repentance and forgiveness can provide important support too, especially when there is sensitivity, patience and openness to the gradual and mutual discovery of realities and truths.

In describing the various factors that contribute to same-sex attractions (also sometimes spoken/written of as "SSA", which indeed presents itself as a condition), this book indirectly shows that efforts by any conservative-religious to "cure", convert, make-straight-again, and "pray away the gay" will not make any headway if these communities do not want to know and reflect on the implications of these factors. Instead, these efforts can cause further distress and harm to those who might already be struggling with questions about attractions and identity. Secondly, this book exposes and explains the reasons and forces behind the silence and non-response of some people in (conservative or religious) authority. This group of people should strive to do what it takes to be the best responders to those who experience same-sex attractions. Unfortunately, however, they seem to often exhibit great reluctance and resistance. The reasons pertain to how homosexuality is connected to morally sensitive people who are affected by various dysfunctions and moral deviances in society, and are therefore more inclined to be religious. Therein lies a hidden irony that needs attention and action, and I hope you will read on to find out more and realise the greater call.

Make no mistake—be aware that there is much more happening beyond just understanding homosexuality. The first chapter gives a glimpse of this. However, I hope the rest of this book will give you more insights to understand the factors within the lives of those who experience same-sex attractions, the very real and heartfelt struggles for those experiencing them first-hand, and also their loved ones and families. I hope you as a community leader, therapist, counsellor, friend or family member will reflect deeply. I hope your hearts will be converted and motivated to attend and heal the myriads of hurt and wounds involved—both consciously and unconsciously. Thereafter, I hope you will be able to play a part in one's journey towards deepening self-discovery wherein they may come to know themselves and their histories more deeply, with a new awareness of what their future can hold. I hope you will understand the greater reason why these issues have arisen. And I hope this endeavour grows into a greater mission that was meant to be. You might then come to understand what Leanne Payne understood, which surprised me initially, and that is when we understand, attend to the needs and remove the sources of hurt of people who have same-sex attractions, we are improving the well-being of the whole of humanity.

Bryan Shen

CHAPTER 1

Terminology, a Prerequisite

It is unusual to start the first chapter with a list of terms. But the many factors and complex ways these interact below consciousness cannot be explained with the limited awareness and terms that an average person has about psychology and phenomenology[1].

It should be of no surprise that when words used are unintentionally nebulous and polysemous (having more than one meaning), then division and polarisation can occur. Thus it is important to begin this book with an explanation of terms, which will help the average person become more aware of things that can happen psychologically below consciousness.

Some of the words may be unfamiliar initially, but that will only be for a while as you read on. Words like "homosexuality", "gay" and "same-sex attractions" are used often in the chapters. I hope you will eventually be familiar with the differences. The words described here are chosen to assist people in conservative-religious communities acquire a better understanding of the issues surrounding homosexuality. The words "intersex" and "gender dysphoria" are used in Chapter 7. Other terms not mentioned further in the chapters but are mentioned here are to give a broader feel of what is going on beyond what a typical conservative-religious community may understand.

Homosexuality—A general term mostly used in clinical, legal, scientific, religious or formal circles/discussions. It can be used in a neutral tone, unlike the word "homosexual", which carries a negative connotation. But in some social environments, it could be used in a derogatory manner. In this book, it is used primarily in reference to the initial stages when a person is in distress or confused, with some awareness of words used disparagingly and with no awareness of the term "same-sex attraction" yet.

Note

It is common for people to use the word "homosexual", along with words like "gay", "lesbian", "SSA", "straight", and sometimes "heterosexual" without going further to distinguish the difference between unchosen attractions and a chosen way of seeing oneself. The words are taken as "one concept" or "one destiny". Effort is required to realise the difference between attractions experienced and self-concept embraced or not-embraced. In many conservative-religious communities, there are far more people with unchosen attractions who do not embrace the self-concepts purported by liberal societies. While I have no objections to those who do, there is an urgent need to go beyond to reach people who are hidden in loneliness and feeling isolated with their unchosen attractions but unconsciously linking it with concepts that are at odds with their faith, culture and community.

Polysemy—A word, acronym or phrase that has more than one meaning. Even though this word is rarely known, a few words or acronyms commonly used in discussions around homosexuality and gender identity are also polysemies. It is important to know the effect of using polysemies because it often causes division and polarisation. An example is the word "Love". In English it has become a polysemy. "Let's make love" and "The love of a parent for a child" do not have the same connotation. This makes phrases like "the right to love" or "Love is love" problematic. It is better to avoid using polysemous words, not only because of the potential for misunderstandings, but also because these can often lead to discord and relational alienation. In this chapter, a few words that are polysemies will be pointed out as they are explained.

Gay—The word "gay" is a polysemy. It entered the English language around the twelfth century with primary meanings of "joyful", "carefree", "bright and showy". From "carefree", it also started to acquire associations of immorality in the fourteenth century. By the eighteenth century, it had specific meanings of "addicted to pleasures and dissipation" and "uninhibited by moral constraints". These were initially associated with heterosexuality (a "gay woman" was a prostitute, a "gay man" was a womaniser, and a "gay house" was a brothel). Even though the word "gay" was not commonly associated with homosexuality in particular (exclusively) until the second half of the twentieth century, the modern gay culture and pride parades also portray, intentionally or not, the earlier associations to "willingness to disregard conventional or respectable sexual mores". The word "gay" today can still be used by both men or women even though in some societies the women identify themselves as "lesbians". The word "gay" can also be used as an adjective ("gay man", "gay bar"), or a noun ("Gays are opposed to the ruling.") and often among teens as a pejorative ("Yuck, that was so gay!").

Sex—Refers to the biological differences between males and females, such as differences in genitalia and chromosome differences, which affect many other subtle aspects, including how males and females neurologically respond to things differently.

Gender—Sense of identity based on social expectations of a male or female, and/or a personal identification of one's own gender based on an internal awareness. It is possible to have a "gender role" while having a different internal "gender identity". In some cultures, social expectations can have a strong bearing. While there are a few cultures that recognise more than two genders, most recognise just two and thus use "gender" and "sex" interchangeably or congruently.

As this book does touch on gender identity development, the word "gender" would be used often in a "congruent to sex" way. This is to highlight how bad role modelling is one factor that can contribute to someone in the next generation having "gender incongruence", where their internal gender identity is not congruent to their sex.

Same-sex attractions—An affective desire for someone of the same sex. Just as opposite-sex attractions are not chosen, same-sex attractions are also not chosen. Just as it is not a sin to one day become aware of one's own opposite-sex attractions, it is not a sin to become aware of one's own same-sex attractions. All religious persons of authority who understand this agree that experiencing same-sex attractions or opposite-sex attractions are not sins. However, acting to take these attractions further into activities like sexually arousing thoughts, using or becoming involved in pornography, fornication and other illicit sexual activity would be considered sins regardless of whether they spring from opposite-sex attractions or same-sex attractions. Being "attractions", they are not necessarily permanent nor are they identities. In some liberal societies, the acronym SSA, denoting Same-Sex Attraction, is taken negatively as a "clinicalised acronym".

Note

We must not to be too quick to label a child as experiencing same-sex attractions or homosexuality as not all attractions are romantic or sexual in nature. It is common for schoolboys or schoolgirls to admire or have "crushes" on a popular star student of the same sex. Most times, the crushes become less consuming as boys and girls imitate their role models and receive affirmation in various ways. Once affirmation is received sufficiently, they begin to notice the opposite sex. Understandably, some individuals do not receive enough affirmation if they are bullied, denigrated, looked down upon, or feel "never good enough" for various reasons including internalised high standards. Correspondingly, these initial crushes do not subside. This then becomes sexualised, leading to homosexual thoughts and even actions after those feelings are connected with sexual feelings, which frequently occur with puberty. (More explanations are in Chapter 3 under "Insufficient affiliation with the same-sex".) The feelings of a person who experiences same-sex attractions are much stronger than a child's "liking a person". There is a sense of being drawn to the person and wanting to be with the person and thinking often of that person. Perhaps it is stronger because the time to "complete being affirmed" has passed and so our deepest "below the conscious" selves, driven by our biology, know there is an urgent need to "step it up".

Gender dysphoria (antonym of euphoria)—A term used by mental health professionals to describe a condition that a person experiences discomfort or distress because there is a mismatch between their biological sex and their internal sense of gender identity. Those in the LGBT community prefer to use the term "transgender" or just "trans". (A "trans male/boy" is born female but wants to be identified as male; and "trans female/girl" is born male but wants to be identified as female. They may want their personal pronouns to be used accordingly.) The feeling can be mild or very strong. Clients may even want to have sex-change operations known as "sex-reassignment surgery", also known as "sex confirmation surgery" in some societies. Gender dysphoria is also sometimes called Gender Incongruence.

Intersex condition—A rare medical condition where a child is born with ambiguous genitalia, neither predominantly male nor female in appearance, due to hormonal dysfunction. (Some explanations are given in Chapter 7.) It is very important not to use the phrase "intersex person" but rather to use the phrase "person with intersex condition".

In the medical profession, the acronym DSD (Disorders of Sexual Development) is more commonly used.

In-born—Characteristics that are present at birth. Medical science today knows a lot about how the health and state of a mother during pregnancy can affect a child profoundly. Therefore, in-born is different from being "God-designed". For example, some gender dysphoria cases have in-born characteristics that are not "designed by God". Furthermore, studies based on self-reporting often give an impression that "earliest memory" equates to "in-born". However, there are important psycho-dynamic factors that often occur between birth and "earliest memory". However, if these distinctions are not made, then this word becomes a polysemy. (The word "innate" is sometimes used interchangeably with "in-born".)

Sexual identity—There are different kinds: homosexuality, bisexuality, polysexuality (attracted to LGBTQ+), pedosexuality, pansexuality (gender-blind), asexuality (not interested in sex), bestiality (zoophilia), etc. These are self-identified according to how one feels and/or what one feels attracted to.

Note

The APA (American Psychological Association) and many people in it now acknowledge that sexual attractions are fluid, and thus sexual identity can change over a person's lifetime. Influential researcher and feminist Dr Lisa Diamond, in her groundbreaking study published in her book, *Sexual Fluidity: Understanding Women's Love and Desire* (2008), maintains that the phrase "born this way" cannot be the endpoint. This does not mean that sexual attractions do not feel innate. There are still complex factors that can happen below consciousness that affect one's sexual attractions.

Paraphilia—Sexual attraction to anything is possible. Each type has a name. Some examples are: paedophilia, hebephilia, infantophilia, frotteurism, gerontophilia, narratophilia, podophilia, pictophilia, raptophilia, transvestophilia, urolagnia and voyeurism. Type "list of paraphilia" in a search engine and you will be able to see that the list is very long: anything under the sun can be sexualised[3].

LGBT (Lesbian Gay Bisexual Transsexual)—This acronym is used to denote a community that advocates acceptance of all types of sexual orientations and gender identities. They often use rainbow colours to denote this diversity. In Singapore, "Intersex" and "Questioning" are added to become LGBTIQ. In Hong Kong, "Intersex" and "Queer" are added to become LGBTIQ. There are many other letters that make the list of self-identified sexual types long—currently over 20. And thus, there are some efforts to acknowledge the many types with acronyms such as LGBTQ+ as this book does. Sometimes it is referred simply as "Community", like in "Community-friendly counselling". Other words can be added, e.g. LGBT movement, LGBT agenda, pro-LGBT legislation, etc. Depending on how this acronym is used, for example in describing specific needs of its member, it often becomes a polysemy.

Affect (noun)—A subjective aspect of feeling or emotion that a person feels, but is unable to compare it in the body of another person, and thus have little awareness of it. For example, if a pair of identical twins witness a surprising event and one twin reacts with surprise and laughter while the other twin reacts with shock and revulsion, their affect is different. And they are not aware of their affect. So one twin could say to the other, "Why are you so negative about it?" while the other twin could say, "How could you laugh at such a thing?" Other examples: When a person has been scolded or looked down upon for a long time, that person has a lot of negative affect, but can unknowingly regard it as "normal". That person may grow up feeling nothing out of the ordinary but is also inexplicably compelled towards being praised, being seen as good, being regarded as worthy (anything that gives positive affect) and would do everything to prevent failure. A person with a lot of negative affect is also more drawn to anything that provides "affect relief" like sex, alcohol, food, shopping, fantasies and pets, among other things.

Pederasty—The pedagogical relationship between an adult male and a pubescent or adolescent male, with a homosexual aspect. This term is mentioned only now in this book. However, it is an important word to know because it exists, more so in Asia, and frequently in "all-male establishments" like the military, scouts, cadet training, religious training houses and certain institutions like ancient Greek-Roman cultures and Japanese Kabukis. An adult male experiencing same-sex attractions (and who may *or may not* self-identify as homosexual) may take a liking to a teenage boy, and offer "elder guidance" or conjure up any form of ploy to eventually have a close intimate (and/or sexual) relationship.

Power differential, desire for grooming and political favour are factors that may influence a boy to consent. Boys who lack affirmation from other males are particularly vulnerable. But if at some point the boy reveals or complains about this behaviour, the presence of pederasty in the system can make intervention, rescue, reporting, therapy and systemic correction extremely difficult, if not impossible. Oftentimes, such systems and organisations will do anything to protect their "good name", including collusion with other authoritative bodies to gas-light[4] both the victim and the rescuer-intervener. Therein lies an example reason why religious authorities like the Vatican find it difficult to detect and deal with the risk of sexual abuse. The risk that is hidden in time arises together with the person who has it (possibly unknowingly) into positions of authority.

The Importance of Using Same-Sex Attractions Correctly

People in conservative-religious communities can easily slip into using same-sex attractions in a polysemous way, especially when uttering the word "gay" or "lesbian" is too cognitively difficult. The word "gay" as it is used today is polysemous. Parents, individuals, friends, pastors, anyone who struggles with these words would be inclined to use same-sex attraction in a polysemous way through unintentional mental word replacement. In the long run, this is harmful because such polysemies create confusion, division and polarisations.

Same-sex attractions should not be converted into an identifier by making it stand for "same-sex *attracted*", enabling ourselves to say "a same-sex-attracted person" like in "influenza-ed person" or "gastritis-ed activities". Identifiers can seal a person in a kind of "destiny". In contrast, a person does not need to have an identity defined by what he or she has or is experiencing. Instead, the spirit of the person can shine regardless of whether they experience opposite-sex attractions or same-sex attractions.

Same-sex attractions should not be used retroactively if it includes feelings of distress, fear, dissonance, anxiety, confusion, etc. If experiencing same-sex attraction is not a sin, then it should not bring distress unless it is misunderstood. I recommend a distinction be made between "experiencing same-sex attractions" and "experiencing homosexual feelings". The first expresses just the attractions without any negative connotations attached to it. For first-person accounts, if feelings attached include distress, fear, dissonance, confusion, etc., then "homosexual feelings" should be used. For example: "I used to struggle with my homosexual feelings. Now that I am accepted and supported by my community even though I still experience same-sex attractions, I find it easier to live a chaste life and I no longer struggle with homosexual feelings." Here are examples of some unintentional errors, and how they can be corrected:

Unintentional erroneous use	Correction
Somehow, being in a religious school made it even more apparent that same-sex attractions (SSA) were a huge taboo. So I stuffed those feelings inside, and went about life.	Somehow, being in a religious school made it even more apparent that having homosexual feelings were a huge taboo. So I stuffed those feelings inside, and went about life.
I had difficulty reconciling the SSA that I felt with my own dream to settle down with a girl.	I had difficulty reconciling the homosexual feelings that I felt with my own dream to settle down with a girl.
Some Christians with SSA have studied the theology regarding this issue very extensively. Some even have strong convictions that the expressions of SSA are against God's will.	Some Christians who experience same-sex attractions have studied the theology regarding this issue very extensively. Some even have strong convictions that the expressions of homosexuality are against God's will.
To hide my SSA from family and other friends, I had to put up a false front.	To hide my experiences of homosexual feelings from family and other friends, I had to put up a false front.
I withdrew deeper into myself due to shame over my SSA and obsessive masturbation. I started having lots of condemning thoughts...	I withdrew deeper into myself due to shame over my homosexual feelings and obsessive masturbation. (I had no idea about separating the same-sex attractions, the feelings, and the act.) I started having lots of condemning thoughts...

Unintentional erroneous use	Correction
He started journeying with me through my SSA struggles.	He started journeying with me through my struggles that came with having same-sex attractions (or opposite-sex attractions).
… thus all of us felt ministered to by being able to share our SSA with each other.	… thus all of us felt ministered to by being able to share with each other our issues that came with experiencing same-sex attractions.
As someone grappling with SSA, I have often felt very alone in my struggles… Indeed, I have not spoken about my SSA to my family and many of my friends.	As someone grappling with same-sex attractions, I have often felt very alone in my struggles… Indeed, I have not spoken about my struggles that come with experiencing same-sex attractions to my family and many of my friends.
I studied at a high school in a conservative society where discussions on SSA were limited and taboo. Teachers would sweep the topic under the rug…	I studied at a high school in a conservative society where discussions on homosexuality were limited and taboo. (Separating same-sex attractions from acting on it or identifying with it was not known to any of us.) Teachers would sweep the topic under the rug…

Unintentional erroneous use	Correction
Siti still struggles with SSA but practises obedience according to what her religion commands.	Siti still experiences same-sex attractions sometimes and occasionally struggles with homosexual feelings, but practises obedience according to what her religion commands. (She hopes to eventually have no more struggles despite having same-sex attractions because of her obedience, and support from her husband and community.)

Note

Experiencing same-sex attractions is something everyone has in some way, whenever they greatly admire someone of the same sex. This occurs frequently in young children and this is a natural part of identity development. Homosexual feelings are something that some people experience when their identity development is affected or delayed by various factors, inclusive of social-cultural ones, as the next few chapters will attempt to explain. Conservative-religious people are likely to associate these feelings with negative-affect and/or consider them sinful. This need not be, as such people need to understand that experiencing same-sex attractions is as challenging as experiencing opposite sex attractions, especially for those who strive to be virtuous. It becomes a problem when they have so much anxiety associated with having these attractions. Just as guidance for people experiencing opposite-sex attractions is beneficial, so would guidance for people experiencing same-sex attractions be beneficial.

Case Stories

The following stories show the importance of knowing the difference between experiencing "same-sex attractions" and "being gay". The first case is quite straightforward. The second case shows how knowing the difference can unravel a case of injustice. The third case shows the importance of not using "same-sex attractions" or its acronym SSA as a replacement polysemy for the word "gay".

Case 1

Zayden is the youngest of three boys. His elder brothers are great role models who did well academically and physically, and both served in the army too. Their religious community was proud of all three of them for being righteous and faithful young men. But Zayden felt "not good enough" despite out-performing his brothers in almost everything. In his final year of high school, a teacher noticed his downcast demeanour and asked if he was alright. He confided that he thought he was gay, and the thought of being a sinner was just too much. During the first counselling session, it took almost 20 minutes to get Zayden to understand the difference between "being gay" and "experiencing same-sex attractions" and that the latter is not a sin. Once he understood, he felt better. His attractions did not lessen, but he did not feel as heavily burdened.

*   *   *

Further sessions established that Zayden had Anxious Attachment and the cause was identified. His brothers' high performance also had an effect. His parents and brothers are now supporting him in informed ways. See Chapter 4 for more explanations.

Case 2

Adam was outed by a religious teacher who told him one day, "I know you are gay". Adam was shocked and wondered how he knew. The teacher had warned Adam to stay away from Jefri (a fellow classmate) but yet he continued seeing Jefri. Adam wanted to clarify that it was Jefri who wanted the friendship. Adam had always ensured that they were never alone. Adam was careful because Jefri was the teacher's favourite student. But it did not matter anymore as the teacher had found out. There are strict rules against homosexuality and now Adam could not continue. The teacher told him that to "avoid the shame," Adam should announce that he had decided not to continue because he was not ready for religious life. After he left, the teacher told his elders privately that Adam was "caught in a homosexual act". Even though that was not true, Adam thought that it did not make any difference since he was gay. He also did not want to raise a fracas with the teacher and the elders.

A year and a half later, Adam went to see a counsellor because he still could not get over his disappointments in life. When he was educated about the difference between "experiencing same-sex attractions" and "being gay", he realised he was not gay even though he had same-sex attractions. Because he had done nothing wrong with Jefri, he decided to lodge an appeal against the wrongful dismissal, pointing out that the teacher had lied about him. This enabled the elders to request a second investigation into the case at a higher level. (The elders too had to be fully educated before they knew what was right and wrong.)

*   *   *

Update: Adam was reinstated, but he had to move to a different province to continue his religious training. The previous province did not want to investigate the false accusation by the religious teacher, saying that it was a "sensitive matter".

Case 3

When Spencer's second child, Ben, aged 32 years, told him and his wife that he (Ben) was gay and was exploring having a partner, both Spencer and his wife were lost for words. It was already hard for them to utter the word "gay", and even harder to link it to their son. In their minds, the word "gay" as a noun or adjective, act or condition, choice or identity, were all the same. In reading up and searching for answers, they found that the acronym SSA was more acceptable in conservative communities than the word "gay". So they began to use SSA in place of the word "gay". Spencer began to say to his son, "Even though you are SSA, there is nothing wrong. You can still love, but you cannot have a gay relationship." But his son's face grimaced in response, and said that Spencer didn't seem to understand.

Spencer, still feeling lost, sought counselling. When asked how long Spencer had been using the acronym SSA, he replied, "Over a year." And when asked if his son ever responded with the acronym SSA, Spencer, after some thought, replied, "No, he never did. He only used the word 'gay' in all his responses." The counsellor said, "Most likely, in your son's mind, the word SSA is just another term for gay. There is no difference in your son's mind. So when you said, "Even though you are

SSA, there is nothing wrong. You can still love, but you cannot have a gay relationship", in your son's mind, it is like hearing you say, "Even though you are gay, there is nothing wrong. You can still love, but you cannot have a gay relationship." He would think that what you said was just nuts." Spencer thereafter took more effort to use same-sex attractions properly, and to take pains to explain its difference with "being gay" to his son. This is a small step towards clarifying and improving understanding between father and son.

Notes

1. Phenomenology is the study of structures of consciousness and objects of experience, while psychology is the study of behaviour and the mind.

2. It is a tragedy that there are some religious persons who actively do not want to know anything about homosexuality. In some cases, such religious persons would even ban educative discussions, talks or books. However, there can be mitigating reasons for why they do this. One of it is that they are in Stage 1 (see Chapter 5 on Stages of Awareness). While they are highly capable and talented (see Chapter 4) and strive very much to do everything right, they are not at all able to attend to what they cannot accept in themselves. It is also a tragedy that some religious institutions are very afraid of, or turn a blind eye to, the fact that there are more people with same-sex attractions in religious training compared to averages (see Chapter 9 for reasons why people who are morally sensitive will more likely be impacted by social factors that contribute to homosexuality).

3. If sexual attraction to anything under the sun is possible (such as attraction to faeces, urine, vomit, pus, mucus, a dead body, a person in pain, an amputee, a tied-in-chains person), it then becomes imperative to know the

dangers of "exploring different sexualities". At the same time, we must keep in mind that it is not inconceivable for someone to develop any kind of paraphilia without intent. And can ignorance of "how pleasure can override wisdom" be without risks? On the other hand, it is beneficial to know well why many religions advocate staying on the "straight and narrow path".

4. Gas-lighting is a form of manipulation that seeks to sow seeds of doubt in a victim or group, to make them question their own memory, perception and understanding. Using persistent denial, misdirection, contradiction, wearing down over time, incongruence, aligning others against the victim, intentional confusion, lying, pointing at others as liars—it destabilises, delegitimises and disorientates the victim(s). It is a common technique of abusers, dictators, narcissists, cult leaders and those in positions of power with something important to hide. The existence of pederasty and gas-lighting in highly respected Asian institutions explains the near total absence of voices of victims, and the presence of a variation of Stockholm Syndrome (see Note 5 below) among victims in order to survive or stay on to climb the ranks, thereby perpetuating the hidden problems.

5. Stockholm Syndrome is a condition that causes victims to develop a psychological alliance with their abusers as a survival strategy in a situation where it seems that no justice can ever be found. These cooperative relationships formed between captor and captives or superior and subordinate during time spent together are generally considered irrational in the light of the danger or risk endured by the captive-subordinate. In some respected institutions, there is an added incentive to "accept it as normal and keep it hidden" because the rewards of maintaining "outward respectability" are huge and sometimes life-long. Generally speaking, it consists of a cooperative relationship that develops between two persons where one person intermittently reminds the other of the consequences of telling the truth.

CHAPTER 2

Gender Identity Development

It is important to understand that a baby's development and the role parents play in the life of the child will have a tremendous effect on the child's early development. It can be positive or negative. It can be good or bad. It is an urgent call to every parent to read and know what makes for normal gender identity development.

The diagram on the next page describes the whole human brain in three evolutionary parts. The Instinctive (Reptilian) Brain deals with survival and reproduction. The Emotional (Mammalian) Brain deals with emotions and parental-relationships. The Thinking (Human) Brain is able to deal with complex logic and abstract thought, including morality, "transcendent God" and "the greater good beyond self".

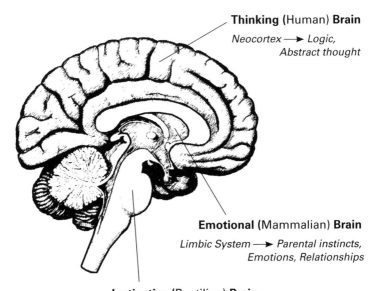

Thinking (Human) **Brain**
Neocortex ⟶ *Logic,*
Abstract thought

Emotional (Mammalian) **Brain**
Limbic System ⟶ *Parental instincts,*
Emotions, Relationships

Instinctive (Reptilian) **Brain**
Basic brain ⟶ *Survival, Reproduction*

By evolution, our instincts can override our emotions and thoughts, and our emotions can override our thoughts. Moreover, our consciousness takes up only 5 per cent of our brain's activity, most of it in the Thinking Brain. Daniel Kahneman, author of the book *Thinking, Fast and Slow*, writes that we use only 5 per cent of our mind for rational thinking. The rest of the time, we rely on our emotions and instincts which are influentially shaped by our early developmental years.

And it begins at conception. A recent research study, published in the *British Journal of Psychiatry*, found that children whose mothers who experience stress or moderate stress while pregnant were three times more likely to develop personality disorders that also affect their ability to socialise. The human brain is very complex, and the three parts need to develop in sequence in a healthy way. In the first six months after birth, the brain grows rapidly as it begins to try to integrate all the senses for the most basic needs: making sense of sights, sound, how to get attention (for food, rest, bodily function), what is danger and what isn't—most of what relates to basic survival.

What needs to develop soon after is the Emotional Brain, which deals with relationships. In this aspect, the first 6 to 18 months of a baby's life is extremely important. Much has been written in the field of developmental psychology. Influential psychologists include Urie Bronfenbrenner, Erik Erikson, Sigmund Freud and Jean Piaget. Stated below are extracts from John Bowlby's work on "Attachment Theory", which was further developed by Mary Ainsworth.

In the first six months, an infant is attached to the mother psycho-emotionally. The baby cannot tell the difference between "being with mummy" and "being mummy". Between 6 months and 18 months, the infant individuates—a boy into the realm of males, and a girl within the realm of females (see diagram on the next page). This coincides with the period where the child begins to crawl and walk, and explore.

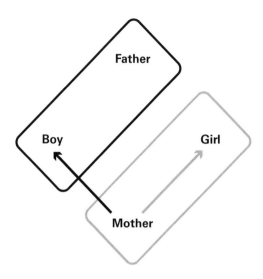

Attachment Style

How a child individuates depends on the kind of "attachment style" that develops during this stage (which relates to the Emotional Brain). This depends on whether the primary caregiver is properly attuned to an infant as he/she attempts to individuate. The crucial dilemma for the child is the "fear of abandonment" versus "individuation". If the primary care-giver is properly attuned, the infant will feel secure knowing that fears, needs and "learning through mistakes" will be properly attended to as he/she explores being a separate individual. This is called a Secure-Attachment Style, which is the normal process.

However, individuation can run into problems depending on the temperament of the infant and the myriad of problems or situations that make the primary caregiver not properly attuned to the infant. If the mother is busy, preoccupied, anxious, troubled or leaves the child-care to someone else who (unknowingly to anyone) is not properly attuned to the child, different attachment styles can develop.

One such style is called the Anxious-Attachment Style, where the child develops an irrational anxiety-laden unsureness of being "not-liked". This can develop into an irrational feeling or fear of being "less favoured".

Another is called the Avoidant-Attachment Style, where the primary caregiver is even more unattuned and/or has too much self-needs and vacillates between oblivious self-occupation and giving attention inappropriately or intrusively. The child's real needs are not attended to, but when the child is able to make his/her real needs known, the caregiver expresses irritation, anger or even punishes the child. This can develop into a fear of being too close in relationships, thus affecting needs for healthy social interactions.

Attachment styles have a profound effect on the child's relationships throughout his/her life. Because attachment style develops during infancy, there is no awareness of it. (Note: This book simplifies the various attachment style terms to just two. Anxious-Ambivalent Attachment and Anxious-Preoccupied Attachment are simplified to

Anxious Attachment. Anxious-Avoidant Attachment and Dismissive-Avoidant Attachment are simplified to Avoidant Attachment. Both these attachment styles are further described in Chapter 4.)

There is another attachment style called the Disorganised-Attachment Style, where the primary care-giver is unpredictable and volatile. The child feels danger but is in a dilemma because "safety from abandonment" is also the source of danger. The effects of this attachment style on homosexuality are not discussed here because of insufficient clinical research, and also in most of such cases, other problems are far more dominant. Last but not least, the primary caregiver's own attachment style will affect the child's individuation process and his/her attachment style—without anyone's awareness.

If a boy is unable to individuate properly from his mother, he may feel more comfortable with his mother than with his father, more with girls than boys, especially if he has difficulties forming an attachment with his father for whatever reason, including bad paternal role modelling. In extreme cases, he may fail to individuate to contain the feeling of "being mummy", as this is more comforting. This is one pathway to gender dysphoria for a male in which attachment is a contributing factor. (Thus gender dysphoria in such cases is typically recalled like, "As early as I can remember, since three years old".)

For a girl, the inability to individuate usually results in the girl assimilating the mother's fears, anxieties, inferior feelings, etc. These can make it harder for the father to enter into the girl's world, made worse if the mother already has a fear of or an emotional distance from the father for whatever reason. These girls can feel insecure and needy, desiring a secure woman who can affirm them.

Note
The two paragraphs above are examples of how attachment issues can contribute to gender dysphoria. However, there are other factors that can also contribute. These other factors are mentioned in Chapter 7.

Post-Individuation

On successful individuation, normally, a boy seeks out his father, who models, encourages, guides, and affirms the boy in ways that anchor his male identity (see diagram below). For the girl, she should see her father providing safety, security and attention to her mother and her. Then she interacts and learns from her mother how to be a woman who gets such attention and security. Together with the mother, the father also provides confirmation-praise, which anchors her female identity.

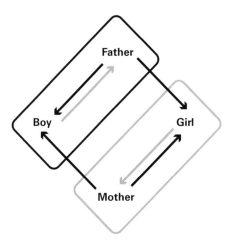

Crucially, the modelling of male and female by the father and mother, their relationship and the example of complementarity between them makes up a three-way affirmation and confirmation of a boy or girl in their respective gender development (see diagram on the following page).

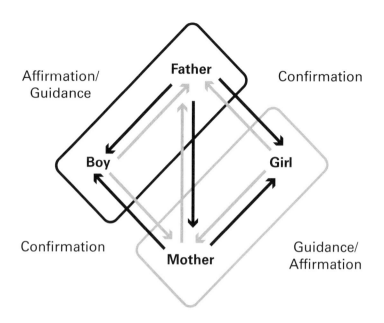

If any part of the triangle is dysfunctional, due to bad relationships between parents or between child and parent, the child may not achieve psycho-emotional wholeness. A child without psycho-emotional wholeness may seek another person of the same sex in an attempt to internalise missing aspects of themselves to feel whole.

Parents who do not respect each other, even though they may not divorce and continue to live together, will still impact the gender identity development of their children. Unfortunately, this is common in some social cultures because "saving face" by showing an intact family is still valued.

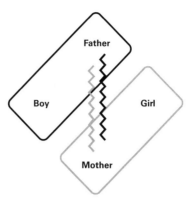

Regardless of how well people outside the family view the family—that it is intact, well-provided for and living the good life—the children know what is going on in the hearts of their parents. A boy will be impacted by his father being devalued, and a girl will be impacted by her mother being devalued. And bad examples or responses from the opposite-gender parent will also impact a child's future relationships with the opposite gender.

For a boy, if the father is a poor role model, or has a bad temper, or does not seem interested, or is too quiet and non-engaging, or leaves all decisions and important matters to his wife, then the boy's outlook, thoughts and view of the world would likely be from the mother's view, attitudes and mind-frame. If he does not have sufficient interaction with other boys and men, then he may be more inclined to be effeminate. This can be further exacerbated if he does not feel he can fit in with other boys, is shunned or bullied by the boys, or if he finds girls more comfortable to be with.

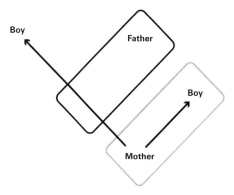

Sometimes the boy is not close to any parent. The possible reasons include parents fighting, both parents being too busy, being in an unhealthy symbiotic relationship, or possessing poor relationship and socialisation skills. The parents' attachment style too can have a significant impact. Such issues may be passed down to the boy. These make him prone to feeling alone, unsure, lacking confidence, etc. These also put the boy at risk of being picked on by bullies. If there is bullying, the boy is often not able to tell his parents. If he does, they are also often not able to respond sufficiently.

The same scenario can happen to girls. They may not like their mothers and/or have a poor relationship with their mothers. Fathers may prove to be more emotionally stable, engaging and comforting. But for girls, the development of same-sex attractions is also more complex and usually includes other factors.

If she sees that being a female is so unappealing or disadvantageous (through poor maternal role modelling or

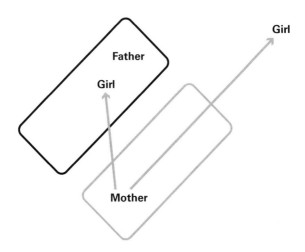

having witnessed mother being weak, used, beaten, etc.), she may subconsciously prefer to identify with the opposite sex, which can be exciting and meaningful or even emotionally safer.

Or she might not like the kind of males and patriarchy around them. Then she may prefer to be "strong, capable, independent and not-needing-men". She can be drawn to feminine-vulnerable females (what she is not) and feel a compulsion to protect them.

She could also not be close to any parent for the same reason that a boy may not be close to any parent. These also make her prone to feeling alone, unsure, a lack of safety or security, etc. While these could drive her to be "strong, independent and capable", it can also make her extra sensitive to negative comments and remarks. Either way, she is often deprived of attention and love, which only becomes clear when it is contrasted, such as when another girl comes, gives her attention, understanding, companionship, acceptance, makes her feel good and confident, with care and insight. It can feel wonderful.

Case 4

Robby is in his thirties. He has a university degree, but has difficulty holding down a job. Since graduating in his mid-twenties, he has held approximately ten jobs. His first job paid well but he hated it. He stuck with it until his education loans were paid up. Then he tried other jobs. But emotions at work were difficult, and he constantly felt bullied. He looks physically fragile and has a pessimistic outlook, yet holds on tightly to his religious faith.

He has a twin sister. Initially, when they went to school together, his sister was his protector. But in high school, she went to a different school while he went to an all-boys school. That was when the bullying became worse. But he did not tell anyone.

At home, Dad was not the kind of person you could talk to. He was busy, driven, got angry easily, and had a philosophy that valued studies and success in career above all else in life. Robby says, "I want to be financially independent from him. And I don't want to be another him." Mum works as an assistant in a government department. She is quiet, neat and keeps her emotions to herself. Their relationship is one where pragmatism rules. Their children were very much left alone to concentrate on their studies.

Robby and his sister were raised by a maid. But from his earliest memory, he felt isolated. He was always in front of the class. He thought: "As long as I do well in studies, I will be alright." This intensified in high school. The more he was bullied, the more isolated he became, and the more he wanted the high grades for the "prestige" it gave because of the low self-esteem he had. Only now in his adulthood does he see that "high grades" did not solve his many problems.

*   *   *

Being attracted to the same sex is the least of Robby's problems. Finding a community, and finding a father figure, are more pressing issues that he needs to survive day by day. He is currently managing with work that involves little social interaction. He sticks close to his religion but does not tell anyone about his struggles. His sister has gone on to be an extremely independent and capable professional. She is not married.

CHAPTER 3

Factors That Contribute to the Development of Same-Sex Attractions

This chapter and the next give a view of what can increase the likelihood of experiencing same-sex attractions.

And these can happen without the person knowing or anyone around them knowing, for that matter. This chapter explains 10 factors that can be determined upon speaking to a person who has same-sex attractions. Unlike the factors to be detailed in the next chapter, these factors, once known, can be recognisable even though they not always are. However, if there is no knowledge of these factors, there is very little chance of knowing that these contribute to experiencing same-sex attractions; even less so if the person does not want to know.

There is much that has been observed in this field of counselling work in Asia. Observations from other professionals have also contributed to the determination of these factors. Some are more prominent in males while others are more prominent in females.

These 10 factors are divided into four groups. None of these factors alone or any combination of these factors can guarantee homosexuality. However, the intensity of factor effects and the number of factors involved raise the possibility.

Note

These factors are derived from clinical observations of clients' intra-psychic perspectives. They are valuable in guiding mental-health professionals to form a unique working hypothesis for each case. We can use the analogy of medical science to describe this:

A doctor is called to help a community in Africa where a medical condition is still not understood, and the only thing known is that factors that cause the condition are complex. Even so, the doctor still has to attend to the patients. The doctor does so with a working hypothesis first, derived from whatever medical precepts he has learnt plus symptoms and information the client can provide. This hypothesis is refined as the doctor gets to know the patient better over time. In the end, the final hypothesis may resemble something known or not. Over time, a pattern with respect to different factors may emerge. With experience, the doctor will build up his/her understanding as well as knowledge of what can be done to reduce the suffering that the condition causes. Over the long run, as other doctors enter the same field of work with more case studies, what could develop are trends, sub-classifications, calls for research, and finally some declared scientific facts.

I believe we are in the beginning stages of understanding homosexuality in a similar way from the viewpoint of psychological science. I hope research in not only these 10 factors but all other factors mentioned in this book can be done comprehensively in due time.

First Group: Intra-Psychic Factors

Intra-psychic factors are difficult to deduce from external observation. Even close friends or parents may not be able to ascertain them. The best way to do so is to interview the person. There are five factors in this group. Any combination of these five factors can give rise to what is also known as "gender non-conforming responses or behaviours".

1. Insufficient affiliation with the same-sex

This means a kind of disaffiliation to the same-sex for any reason, including poor gender-role modelling by others of the same-sex. (The word "gender" is used congruently here with "sex" to highlight that it is the bad effects of certain "gender expressions" that can cause same-sex disaffiliation.) A poor relationship with the same-gender parent[1] and/or siblings is a common example. Sometimes, even periodic fights or disagreements are enough to maintain a feel of "I can never get along with him/her". Abuse or neglect by same-gender parent can also heighten the disaffiliation.

Another major cause is the situation where the individual is the victim of bullying by classmates, same-gender siblings, and any behaviour that is derogatory by others of the same gender. With social media, this can be done remotely in concerted ways by groups, cliques and gangs. And it is all the worse if the target victim is lonely, isolated, has little connection with parents, or has parents who are too occupied to be aware, among other reasons.

The disaffiliation can also arise where an individual may not like the behaviour of others of the same gender, for any reason. He/she could be a witness, or a victim, of injustice in society or at home, or sees the silence or apathy of adults of the same gender. If a person's perceived social, cultural or religious status is too elevated (or sometimes, too poor), disaffiliation can also occur.

A common question asked is, "How does same-sex disaffiliation lead to same-sex attraction?" The answer lies in two levels of the mind (the Thinking Brain and the Emotional Brain; see diagram on page 22). A child, from toddler age—normally—would have a deep unconscious biologically driven natural need to look at role models of the same sex. This is called the "gender-identity development" phase, which should help to complete the task of affirming the child in his/her gender by puberty. Little boys may say, "I want to go with daddy", "I want to be like Superman!" or "Wow! Maverick in *Top Gun* is so cool!" or "I want to go camping with the guys too". Little girls might say, "Oh! That actress is so attractive!" or "Wow! That girl is so smart!" That is not all. There is also role play or imitation—boys might want to play soldiers and girls might want to play house. Crucially, the child has to receive signs of affirmation from people of the same gender, verbally or more importantly through non-verbal ways that is received through intuition. Even experiencing no objection from others can be valid forms of affirmation. All of these occur at a deep subconscious level—at the Emotional Brain.

If at the conscious level, however, there is too much dis-affirmation—through reasons described earlier—then disaffiliation can occur. In most cases, this disaffiliation does not override the deep unconscious natural drive to look at role models of the same gender, but it delays its completion. Instead of completing its task of affirming a boy/girl in his/her gender, this drive carries on into and past puberty. When it gets sexualised, only then does the awareness or worry of having homosexuality occurs. This also explains why often, when a gay person says, "I've felt like this since seven years old; a few years before puberty", it is frequently in retrospect.

2. Gender incongruence

Gender incongruence refers to feeling different from people of the same gender. There is a shortfall between the perception of self and that of what persons of the same gender should be. (The word "gender" here is also used congruently with "sex". The "gender expressions" that are observed are desirable, but the observer feels the shortfall in himself or herself .) This may mean feeling odd, excluded, "not-good-enough", "defective", "I don't matter", "non-existent", "too different", etc., compared to others of the same gender.

It can happen if a boy thinks a man should be muscular like Superman, but he is thin and scrawny. Or if he admires guys who are good at sports, but he is clumsy in sports. Or a girl who thinks that girls should be like Barbie dolls, but she is fat and pudgy. Or if she admires girls who are smart and confident, but she feels inadequate and lacks self-confidence.

Importantly, what affects one is the perception, not reality. If a boy is neither thin nor clumsy, but he has been decried often by a parent for being so, or if a girl is not pudgy or silly but a parent constantly says so, then gender incongruence can still exist.

Being bullied frequently makes these feelings feel real and "confirmed". Having Anxious-Attachment style also frequently exacerbates this because such people are often extra fearful of not-being-liked. They often have feelings of "I should be better at (this and that)", adding to gender incongruence.

3. Unhealthy relationship(s) with the opposite gender

This includes instances where a boy/girl is abused physically, verbally and emotionally by someone of the opposite gender. In the case of a girl, she could be outraged or turned off by bad examples of boys and men. For a boy, he could be receiving emasculating words or messages from females around him, including classmates, siblings or even his own mother. For a girl, she could be receiving unwanted attention from boys and/or men that makes her feel very uncomfortable over time. Husbands who are poor role models are also a common problem. Moral sensitivity also increases the likelihood of being negatively affected, sometimes without any instigation whatsoever. Some teenagers also develop an aversion to the opposite gender when their morality grows in tandem with religious instruction. This may be because of unhealthy relationships they had with someone of the opposite gender when they were young but did not feel bad about it at that time as their morality had not matured yet.

Case 5

John Carlo, the eldest of three boys, is in his mid-twenties. His father, a quiet man with limited education, is a handyman. His mother, on the other hand, has risen to a high position in an international corporation in their country's capital city. Although she is extremely generous in giving gifts and lavish meals, she also often gives emasculating remarks poorly disguised as attempts to drive men around her to "do better". It seems to work in her company office. But the impact on her husband reduces him to silence and passive-aggressive responses. This tends to result in frequent fights erupting in front of their children.

John Carlo has been shamed by her many times, "There you go again doing things in a *bakla* way" (a local derogative word for effeminate boys) or "You are a loser-boy!". She would ask him to perform a dance or sing a song and then giggle with her friends when he did. Her reactions would be far worse if she felt offended. Once, at home, after John Carlo made a comment that upset her, she chased him into the washroom, cornered him and poked him repeatedly with a broom-stick at his genital area saying, "What are you going to do now, loser-boy? What are you going to do now?"

John Carlo was brought up by his maternal grandmother, whose character is the same as his mother's: loud, fierce, strict and very much "in-your-face". Grandmother also cooked delicious food. Just as mother was "generous and lavish" with money, grandma was "generous and lavish" with food, perhaps as a way to compensate for any emotional hurts. The children were often in an emotional bind. John Carlo stayed with grandma until high school. He was overweight. In school, boys would play the game of "who could touch his genitals then outrun him". Many could.

John Carlo struggles mightily with his desire and longing for men who look better than him. At work, he is easily discouraged by expectations. He has good talent in presentation and speaking, and his ideas and work standards are very high. But he feels ignored by office colleagues. He eats lunch alone. He strongly believes in the precepts of his religious faith. He has a girlfriend of the same faith who knows about his struggles that come with experiencing same-sex attractions. She is his main supporter. But he has not yet told his parents about his struggles with those attractions.

He has a younger brother who is openly gay and has left their family's religious faith. And his youngest brother, who is very sensitive and quiet, has a girl-friend who is domineering and emasculating as well. The combination of his mother's narcissistic personality, voiceless father figure, gender shaming, bullying, and many other factors all contribute to a much higher probability of gender identity developmental problems than any "homosexuality is caused by biology" theory. All her children are affected. But she says, "My family is not that bad. Other families are worse."

4. Relationship(s) with the opposite gender is dominant

(Some of these explanations have been covered in the previous chapter, but they are reiterated here to underscore the importance of this factor.)

A mother-son relationship can be close for a variety of reasons. The father may be emotionally distant, or he may be excessively strict, harsh and critical to the boy. If the father is emotionally, verbally or physically abusive to the mother, the boy may draw closer to her too. On the other hand, if the mother is domineering, the boy may (unconsciously) choose to be close to her to remain safe or "on her good side".

Sometimes the boy is emotionally close to a sister, or has a sister with a dominant influence. Or, because of bullying in school, he has predominately female friends as he feels safe and comfortable with girls. This can be made worse if the boy feels inadequate in sports and feels unwanted by any boys team.

A boy may have an even closer relationship with his mother if there was failure to individuate as a toddler (described earlier on page 26, last paragraph). This can happen for a variety of reasons that causes a mother's emotional state to make the bond between mother and baby very close. A medical condition in either the boy or mother could cause this. An ambivalence-laden anxiety about her husband's fidelity could also cause this.

For a girl, if a close father-daughter relationship has a healthy admiration and respect for the differences between males and females, same-sex attractions frequently do not develop. The same if she has many brothers, or if she is the only girl among the boys. However, if she perceives there is a preference for boys, or if there is an unhealthy patriarchy among males, and there is also an anxiety in her to not feel neglected, denigrated or unworthy, then she might have an unconscious focus to be "better than a woman"; to be "gender non-conforming".

A girl may not have a close relationship with her mother for a variety of reasons. If she sees her mother being treated as a second-class human, and her mother accepting it as "fate", she might feel an abhorrence to being a woman in such a society. The same could happen if she has sisters. The problem can be made worse if other girls reject her for not being "like one of them", or for not being "girly enough". It can exacerbate when cruel words about her are being passed verbally and through social media.

And if the girl with the above situation starts receiving praises for breaking female gender boundaries with success, it can feel good, wonderful and emotionally fulfilling, which soothes the underlying anxiety that drives her to succeed. However, unknowingly, this also detracts from her experiencing (not just knowing) a comfortable relaxed enjoyment of men and of admiring men—which does not preclude her from achieving what she can as a woman. The difference is that she need not succeed alone, and she need not compete against men or do so to prove something. She can do so with a deep feeling that there are men who support, admire, respect and value her as a woman, and not as a lesser human or as some kind of male-replacement.

5. Gender concept distortion

Gender concept distortion is when a male is perceived as superior/inferior, or the female is perceived as inferior/superior, thus giving rise to the perception that the male and female are perceived as not complementary to each other. This can develop when parents are fighting and the father may say to a child, "All women are b*tchy like that!" or the mother may say, "All men are horrible and cannot be trusted!" This can affect a child's own gender identity development or a child's ability to relate correctly with the opposite sex.

It can also develop when a child witnesses terrible consequences happening to their elder siblings for having a boyfriend or girlfriend (in a heterosexual relationship). So, unknown to others, the "good child" has gender concept distortion and subconsciously maintains it to stay "good".

Not uncommonly, a mother's misandry is often silent but passed down to their children. Her daughter could be extra cautious or suspicious of men. Her son could be convinced to avoid other boys. On the other hand, preference for sons (common among South Asians) or maternal favouritism for boys (common among traditional Chinese) can cause a myriad of issues in girls. These issues can in turn perpetuate from one generation to another and contributes to gender identity developmental problems, which may or may not be expressed due to cultural-religious disapproval, prejudice, etc.

Second Group: External Factors

6. Sexual conditioning

Sexual conditioning refers to the early exposure of the child to inappropriate sexual behaviour and pornography by friends/relatives of the same gender, including sexual grooming. Other factors include weak or ineffective moral instruction from parents, leading to a lack of moral defences and a lack of awareness of the benefits of the virtue of chastity. In today's world, where the mass media is increasingly sexualised and easily accessible by ever younger children, the teaching of moral defences and the benefits of the virtue of chastity has to be done sooner and more consistently in order to be more effective. Unfortunately, insufficient attention (and the presence of unscrupulous marketing) has markedly increased a child's likelihood of growing up with increasingly "liberal" social attitudes, which may lead the child to enter addictive sexual behaviours, including homosexual ones.

7. Sexual abuse, physically, mentally or morally

It is important to state what sexual abuse is with reference to gender role modelling. Sexual abuse is any act, gesture, word, sound, posture, or a combination of any of these that conveys a sexually immoral intention perceived by the intended victim. No physical touch, fondling or penetration is needed for the victim to be negatively affected. The following are some examples: A man intentionally slurps his lips in a provocative gesture to a woman who is obviously uncomfortable and fearful. A teacher (of any gender) attempts to slide his/her hand into the pants of a boy but is unable to because the boy swipes the hand off. A teenager flashes a centre-fold of naked bodies to a girl and she covers her face in horror. If the perpetrator is of the same gender with the victim, then same-gender disaffiliation may develop. If the perpetrator is of the opposite gender, then the victim may not be able to develop a healthy and respectful relationship with the opposite gender. These can impact the development of a child's understanding of gender roles and perception of gender identity.

What is more poignant is that abuse may not cause any problem in the child's early years but negative affects can arise later in life. This is because a child's morality usually matures later. Many studies report that up to 90 per cent of perpetrators[2] are known to the child. A child's immature morality makes it easy for perpetrators to "groom" or prepare (through brain-washing) a child for the abuse (which is often not interpreted as abuse by the child, possibly because they are made to feel special and chosen in many ways leading up to it). Not uncommonly in such cases, abuse can be repeated. In later years, when the child's maturing morality realises the abuse as a violation, then the negative affects begin. Perpetrators of whom the general public expects higher morality, inflict greater harm. These include parents, respected elders, religious figures, teachers, and anyone who purports to be good and upright. A young child may initially trust and believe in them. But when their morality matures and catches up, the negative effects caused by the abuse are heightened by the realisation of betrayal and hypocrisy. This can be made worse when the perpetrator denies, lies, gaslights, and/or aligns others against the victim. The impact on the child's gender identity development is then made worse.

Victims can also reveal the abuse to other people. But if these people, who should respond with justice, choose to disbelieve, trivialise, accuse the victim of lying, or collude and cover for the perpetrator, then the negative affects are also made worse. These people could be spouses, colleagues or superiors (of the perpetrator) who could stand to lose a lot if truth and justice were to prevail. When truth and justice are suppressed, while a sense of moral violation remains and impunity continues, then the child may not only have gender identity problems but also develop other symptoms of dysfunction, because the child's own moral development is severely impacted by bad role models. Yet, this can be further made worse if they are decried by the very same people who should have responded with justice but did the opposite.

Children who are exposed to, or have access to, moral-religious instruction are also more likely to grow to feel the negative affects of any form of sexual abuse, past or present. Conversely, giving up or not having moral-religious instruction can reduce the sense of violation among sexual abuse victims, even though this does not solve or remove any of the resultant dysfunction. In a society where little attention is paid to immorality, truth and justice, moral-religious instruction brings uncomfortable encumbrances unless it is taught in shallow ways. All these may explain why the number of people practising their religious faith is plummeting in tandem with people wanting to join religious life.

Third Group: Biological Contributions

8. Biological and physical factors

There are some biological and physical factors that increase predisposition towards experiencing same-sex attractions, but do not predetermine it. These include any physical attributes that increases a child's sense of being odd or "not good enough". Children with "not-obvious medical conditions" that make it harder for the child to "keep up with the others" can be exacerbated if the child feels like he/she "must keep up".

Exposure to chemicals and stress during pregnancy that increases the sensitive temperament of a child could play a role in increasing the predisposition. Studies are currently being conducted to investigate the links. Severe stress experienced by a mother during pregnancy is known to increase the risk of poor mental health in the child.

It is important to note that there are children who may be biologically predisposed (e.g. weak and sensitive boys) but do not develop same-sex attractions due to healthy psycho-familial-social factors. And there are children who are not biologically predisposed (e.g. physically masculine boys) but do develop same-sex attractions due to unhealthy psycho-familial-social factors. There are many clinical cases of these.

Fourth Group: Other Factors

9. Certain personality traits

Any personality traits inclusive of some attachment styles that limit or make it difficult for the child to socialise or interact with others of the same gender, either in school or otherwise, can increase the possibility of experiencing same-sex attractions. Examples include introversion, suspiciousness, social awkwardness, shyness, preference for solitary activities and a negative attitude to a society shaped by cultural or familial beliefs, which can be passed down from generation to generation. A certain level of neuroticism, paranoid thinking, tendency to ruminate, fear of offending others and depression can all contribute too. Children with such personality traits are also often targets of bullying and derision in school or in the neighbourhood. This bullying and derision itself can trigger and worsen these personality traits, especially if experienced by a young child.

Certain situations or home environments can encourage more of such personality traits. These include children placed in institutional homes because of difficult family situations or personal challenges. They will be more at risk of personality problems as well as factors that can affect their gender identity development. It is of great importance that caregivers of these homes and institutions are in sufficient numbers, have the right heart and have adequate training.

Straddling between personality traits and biological factors (mentioned in the previous group) are certain illnesses that are biologically related. Populations with bipolar disorder, borderline personality disorder (BPD) and schizophrenia also have high percentages of people who experience same-sex attractions. It is possible that the attractions result not from these conditions but from how society reacts to these conditions being present in them. These can compound and multiply the person's sense of feeling isolated, derided, not-good-enough, feeling odd and that "everyone is against me".

10. Insufficient occupation with reality

One other factor that perhaps could overlap with factor number 9 above, but is observed often enough in some clients, is an imaginative/creative mind. Sometimes a child does not engage much in actual social interactions with other children or people of the same gender because of various reasons, including being easily wounded due to a sensitive nature, or being prohibited by family or cultural circumstances. They may describe their childhood as, "I like to play pretend games" or "being in an alternate world" or "I like reading fiction stories" or "having a creative imagination". Some children do so to compensate, consciously or not, for the loss of social interaction. In extreme cases, it may be a form of escapism from the stress of the (family or home) situation they are in. Loneliness may not be far from their consciousness. Some children are actually happy to be in an imaginative world. However, in doing so, they may not have enough real interaction with others of the same sex. This may lead to a decreased ability to bond healthily with same-sex peers at a young age, which may lead to feeling that they are unlike the others. All these contribute towards the development of same-sex attractions. It may contribute to the reasons why the creative and entertainment industry seems to have a larger proportion of people who experience same-sex attractions and who self-identify as gay.

Case 6

Ravi is a well-built, physically fit and good-looking young man in his early twenties. He is also intelligent, witty, articulate, dependable, responsible and always ready to take the lead if required. Moreover, Ravi has always been interested in spirituality and morality. His interest in these was because of his paternal grandmother, whom he was raised by and is very close to. His father is also very good-looking, but he was a womaniser. His mother was still a college student when Ravi was born. She was from a high-class family. So it is not known if her parents knew about Ravi or if they did not want to know, even until today. That was why Ravi was taken in and raised by his paternal grandmother. About three years after his birth, his mother stopped visiting him. He never saw her again. His father in the meantime continued his womanising while working out of town, and many years later married and settled down in another town. He was not close to Ravi.

Grandma was an upright pious lady. She taught him the prayers, practice of the faith and guided him in what is right and to avoid wrong. She was also respected in her religious community. Grandpa on the other hand had a drinking problem, as did many of the men in the town where they lived. Grandpa was often called out by his friends who got him drunk—about twice a week.

When grandpa was drunk, Ravi and grandma had to avoid him, sometimes sneaking out of the house. Ravi was not allowed to play with the children in the neighbourhood. Grandma did not want him to be badly influenced. But he did not feel deprived. Grandma ran a small cottage industry from home where she employed a few ladies. They often brought their daughters and Ravi had them to play with. He was lively and talkative. At other times, he watched TV or played in his imagination.

When he was around 10 years old, people around him started saying he was gay. Even though it was always said more in jest, Ravi hated it. But he remained a lively student, active in volleyball and in the school debate team. One day, a male teacher who taught the class music came in with a song that he had written. The song was a comedy about gay people. There were five verses. The last line of each verse was the punchline. Unfortunately, Ravi's name was mentioned before the singing started. During the first verse, the whole class (of about 40 students) were looking at him in anticipation. At the punch-line, they all burst out laughing, and he burst out crying. But the song went on and on, verse after verse.

It was an extremely hurtful memory to recall. Ravi still says, "I hate it. I hate it so much when people say that I am gay." And after a long silence, he adds with a huge sigh, "But I am!" He is currently studying in a religious school, working towards ordination. He is also interested in educating the young.

* * *

Common factors in such cases like Ravi's are: a strong morality instilled by a close female, usually a mother and/or grandmother, plus poor father figures. Other contributing factors include predominant childhood play with girls, poor male role models and an imaginative mind. Being made fun of made things worse. Not knowing the difference between "being gay" and "experiencing same-sex attractions" also added to the distress.

Two Criteria

More than a few factors can exist in a person with same-sex attractions. Each factor on its own may or may not be the main factor contributing to same-sex attractions. Yet, many factors can interact in complex ways that can tip the balance, pushing the person further towards experiencing same-sex attractions. But even then, there may be social and cultural reasons that can suppress it. In Chapter 6, the stages of awareness of same-sex attractions will illustrate how this can be. But while we are still in this chapter, a distinction between the attraction and the erotic sexualisation of the attraction has to be made.

The first criterion is a strong compulsion to look at, or be drawn to, persons of the same sex because of attributes they find attractive.

For males, certain aspects of other males would often catch their attention: good looks, a good body, a kind of "purity", sometimes a fatherly figure, sometimes a younger boy, often the same age, someone athletic, someone confident and smart, etc. (They might not be aware that what they are attracted to indicates an aspect of themselves that is missing or yet to be affirmed.)

For females, things are usually more complex. It could be a frequent urge to look for a sense of worth or value (with an unconscious ignoring of the possibility of feeling worthy and valuable without effort because of men. This may be because of numerous bad examples of men in their lives—e.g. bad patriarchy). For females, it can also be a desire to look out for and care for girls who feel vulnerable, unvalued, unworthy, lack confidence, lack awareness of their own potential, etc.

The second criterion is sexualisation. This is the connection between these aforementioned feelings, urges and compulsions, and anything that is interpreted as sexual. Usually, this would naturally happen when puberty starts. But it can also happen earlier if society is highly exposed to sexualised images and constant titillations.

It is possible to have these feelings, urges and compulsions, and not have them sexualised. This is common in pre-pubescent children. In some conservative (Asian) communities, sexualisation in teenage boys may occur late, and for some of their girls, it may never be sexualised. But the current social/media trends increasingly facilitate sexualisation of all sorts of things and at an earlier age.

Case 7

Tabitha was already in her late sixties when I met her. Maybe it was because I said I was a counsellor that she shared more than she normally would. Her children are well into their adulthood, some into parenthood.

Eight years ago, Tabitha's youngest child, in his late twenties, graduated with a Master's degree. Immediately, he asked her permission to marry his fiancée of two years. He was not only close to Tabitha but was also an upright, sensitive and properly brought-up son that any mother would be proud of. She gave her permission, and an engagement day was arranged. His fiancée's parents were delighted because they liked him very much and thought he would be great for their daughter. The engagement was held at Tabitha's home. Both parents met for the first time. It was a happy occasion that lasted well into the night. There was so much to look forward to.

Three weeks later, Tabitha's son hanged himself. There was no suicide note, and no sign of depression or psychosis. He had some worry about not being able to complete his work, but he had had such worries before. There was nothing to indicate anything serious. Tabitha was more than lost. He was very close to her. She drove him to school and back every day. They had close conversations. Even after eight years, she still feels his presence in the car. So many other things they did together remind her of him. And she still does not know why he took his life.

When I asked about her husband and what role he played in his children's life, she sighed in lamentation. "When my children were younger, my husband was abusive and violent. He had a bad temper. He was also not faithful, having affairs with women. More importantly, he was violent to me and my children saw it. My two daughters and son begged me to leave him. I was on the verge of leaving him when he had an accident. He was hospitalised and came back crippled in a wheelchair. I decided not to leave him. But he continued to be abusive and difficult to me and my children. I did everything I could to lead my children on the right path. And my son wanted very much to do what is right and not be like my husband."

* * *

Being sensitive and with a high sense of morality, Tabitha's son was impacted by a father who was the opposite of the values he held dear. His core self as a male was not affirmed by a father figure. Tabitha recalled times in his younger years when he felt "not good enough" and seemed to be in distress. And she wondered if something similar came up to tip him over. There was no homosexuality. He never agreed with it. His high morality would not allow it. He had huge empathy for anyone who suffered in silence or discrimination. He was well-liked by all his friends. So the hypothesis is: it was his sense of "lack of value" deep in his core that was driving his high sense of "doing good" (see Chapter 4 for explanations). Unfortunately, without anyone knowing, any praise he got only reinforced his belief that only if he succeeded in doing good would he be valued. So, any situation that he was in charge of, that seem to fall behind and "not succeed", would fill him with severe dread. Many people who experience same-sex attractions or who self-identify as gay commonly have this as part of their lives.

*   *   *

Tabitha took time to understand all that had happened. She has support from many people, and has slowly come to be at peace. Her son's friends have remained close to her. She feels blessed by them and their growing families. And she has a strong desire to be there for any young adult who feels "not good enough".

Homosexuality in Animals

Bruce Bagemihl's stunning book, *Biological Exuberance: Animal Homosexuality and Natural Diversity*, is extremely detailed. Published in 1999, it brings together chronicles of 200 years of observations by many professionals in the field of studying animal behaviour. According to Bagemihl, the animal kingdom engages in homosexual behaviour "with much greater sexual diversity—including homosexual, bisexual and non-reproductive sex". The sheer variety is staggering, even weird and bizarre to us humans.

Chapter 2 of Bagemihl's book is titled "Humanistic Animals, Animalistic Humans", in which he comments about our propensity to project human behaviour onto animals and vice-versa. He writes: "Observer after scientific observer has commented how homosexual behavior in animals is greeted with nonchalance from nearby animals. Individuals move effortlessly between their homosexual activities and other social interactions or behaviors without eliciting so much as a second glance from the animals around them." Referring to the diagram on Chapter 2 (page 22), we realise that animals do not have a developed Neocortex, as a human brain does, which is required for morality and conscience. I would postulate that homosexuality has more to do with the Emotional Brain, which includes the Instinctive Brain. Emotions are adaptive according to the "social-relational situation" and individual experiences. This adaptability can be both a benefit and a bane. This can explain why homosexuality can exist in animals and why nonchalance is widespread among them. Referring to the diagram again, we can see how it is possible for two animals of the same sex, like penguins, to have parental instincts.

Paul L. Vasay, in his book, *Homosexual Behavior in Animals: An Evolutionary Perspective* (2006), wrote: "While homosexual behavior is widespread among our primate relatives, aggression specifically directed towards individuals that engage in it appears to be a uniquely human invention." I believe the reasons for such aggression are far more complex than just a "human invention"; it also involves triggers in the limbic system of the brain. However, I would also put forth that it is not beyond human minds to understand the complexities in a comprehensive way to preclude aggression, prejudice, hurtful remarks and discrimination, as well as to reduce the dissonance and struggles that many people have internally and in society. As a human race, I think it's imperative that we do.

Notes

1. If this disaffiliation is very strong through extreme circumstances, then a disavowal of one's own gender may occur, which can overpower the deep natural drive. This is one factor that contributes to gender dysphoria. But as with same-sex attractions, gender dysphoria frequently includes other factors described in this chapter and the next.

2. From the US Department of Justice, an estimated 60 per cent of the perpetrators of child sexual abuse are known to the child but are not family members, e.g., family friends, babysitters, child care providers, neighbours. About 30 per cent of the perpetrators of child sexual abuse are family members. Only about 10 per cent of the perpetrators of child sexual abuse are strangers to the child. Taken from <https://www.nsopw.gov/en/Education/FactsStatistics?AspxAutoDetectCookieSupport=1> on 15 June 2018. Other sources include <https://www.d2l.org/the-issue/statistics/>.

CHAPTER 4

Why Are People With Same-Sex Attractions Often So Talented?

Following the 10 factors described earlier, an over-focus on high standards and morality could be the eleventh factor in the previous chapter. However, I have decided to dedicate this whole chapter to explain not just how it manifests but, more importantly, why it arises.

Not every talented person has same-sex attractions, but it is common for such people to be seen as talented, capable, high-performers, perfectionists and achievers. People around them often notice it. Yet, many people who experience same-sex attractions do not feel good enough deep inside. Some can be surprised when they are told, "You are so good at (this and that)." Some desire success so much that they may get very flustered with working relationships that don't seem to be assuring enough in reliability and quality. Some prefer to work alone, spending inordinate amounts of effort, time and attention to detail. Those who successfully reach high levels may still need a lot of assurance that they are good.

They are also highly sensitive to perceived slights and negative regards.

At their core, below consciousness (within the inner circle of the diagram below) is a combination of any of the three aspects described below. These are the drivers of their high talent.

1. A constant deep feeling of being "not good enough".
2. A dread/fear of being humiliated, denigrated, shamed, admonished, being regarded negatively.
3. A kind of negative void. There is no core worthiness. The person's sense of value is in their talents, achievements and high performance. So they may not even be aware of an "inner absence of affirmation" that needs the presence of their outer "praise-worthiness".

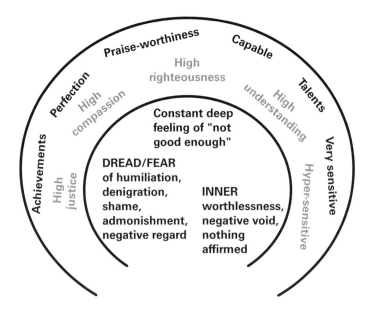

It is this core—of not being affirmed in a visceral sense—that contributes to experiencing same-sex attractions. It is the un-affirmed core in a human being. Not everyone who has such a core will have homosexuality, but the vast majority of those experiencing same-sex attractions do not have sufficient affirmation as a person congruent to their deepest self that is intricately linked to their biological selves. In a human, a vastly complex bio-neurology drives deep psychological needs towards socialisation and procreation needs.

A young boy will have natural drives to observe males, emulate good role models, and be affirmed by other males before he possesses—deep below his consciousness—a relaxed and secure outward-looking disposition that can also recognise that there is an exotic version of his own gender. (Refer to Chapter 3 under "Insufficient affiliation with the same-sex" for how disaffiliation at the conscious level may not allow this to occur below consciousness. Keep in mind that there are other factors that contribute to homosexuality.)

A young girl not only has the same drives to feel affirmed, but also needs to feel secure in the presence of males with stronger testosterone-driven physicalities. Thus, if she also feels unsafe due to bad male role models, bad patriarchy, and/or feels that she has to fend for herself, she would have difficulty feeling properly valued in a relaxed and secure way. This is why many who experience same-sex attractions feel they do not need men to feel safe or valued.

Whether heterosexual or not, people with un-affirmed cores often have problems in relationships. For those who experience same-sex attractions, an attractive same-sex other person has the outward manifestations of what the admirer intuitively feels will fulfil what is missing in his/her core. Often, the admirer is not even aware of what is missing in himself/herself, because the self is not aware of what the self does not have. And this is the part that the self cannot give in a same-sex relationship. It is also true that heterosexuals with such a core will have problems in their relationship with their partners. And they will also have problems giving what they do not have to their children.

There are a number of reasons that can cause these three aspects to exist at the core. These are shown in dashed-grey boxes in the diagram on the next page, and described in three groups as follows.

a. The first "group of reasons" is *shaming, abuse of any kind, and bullying*, which gives rise to the various aspects as described earlier. How these can do so is obvious. The previous chapter also covered some factors that fit into this group of reasons. In addition, abuse that comes from lack of compassion, lack of understanding, immorality and injustices can drive the victim to desire very much the qualities of compassion, understanding, righteousness and justice. They are very sensitive to the lack of these—even

1. **Presence of Competition**   3. **Perceived Expectations**
2. **Comparable Likeness** (culture, family, siblings, twins)

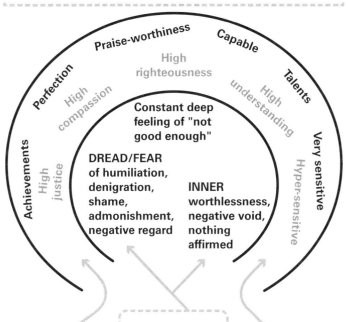

Praise-worthiness   Capable

Perfection   High righteousness   Talents

High compassion   High understanding

Achievements   Very sensitive

High justice   Hyper-sensitive

Constant deep feeling of "not good enough"

DREAD/FEAR of humiliation, denigration, shame, admonishment, negative regard

INNER worthlessness, negative void, nothing affirmed

Hyper-afraid of "*he/she/they won't like me*" so I preempt with these outer qualities to make them like me.

Shaming, abuse (physical, emotional, verbal, sexual, injustice) bullying.

Hyper-afraid of showing "*I've got problems; I have needs,*" so I show *I'm competent and independent.*

Anxious Attachment Style

Avoidant Attachment Style

though they do not know what the presence of these are. If they have suffered unfair denigration for the most part of their lives, they avoid it by acting out what they think people around them want to see.

Shaming may sometimes be done to chastise a person with good intentions. So while it may not be perceived as a bad thing, it can unintentionally maintain the inner worthlessness while encouraging outer praise-worthiness. This is especially so if family and/ or people around them were raised in the same way. This is pointed out not to lay blame but to highlight the importance of learning to distinguish between intrinsic value and outer value, and to affirm accordingly in better ways.

b. The next "group of reasons" pertains to attachment styles. Two types are mentioned here.

   Anxious-Attachment Style: The person with it constantly feels a deep inexpressible threat of being abandoned or rejected, and so concludes that "I'm not good enough" or "I'm less favoured" or "if I don't do (this and that), I will not be loved". It can be so strong that despite tangible proof of high-performance, good behaviour and achievement, the person still feels "not good enough". Having Anxious-Attachment Style does not mean the person will go on to have same-sex attractions because it does exist in heterosexual relationships too. But it can be a powerful multiplier to other factors that contribute to experiencing same-sex attractions.

Avoidant-Attachment Style: The person with it has to show independence, competence, "I don't need any help; I am fine, and everything is fine." This may come from a childhood where expressing a need is met by painful disappointment, disdain or even punishment. Being competent and independent is needed to survive. But they are often not aware of their deep inner needs and bodily needs too. They are not at all aware that there is supposed to be an intrinsic sense of worthiness. It is also not uncommon for people with Avoidant-Attachment Style to have been abused during childhood, so they feel uncomfortable being close in relationships. These acts of abuse also increase various aspects at the core that drive up competence as well as contribute to experiencing same-sex attractions.

c. The last "group of reasons" pertains to anything that can unintentionally cause "inner absence of affirmation"[1]—for example, if there is presence of competition (examples of high-performers exists) and there is "comparable likeness" (same culture, same family, siblings, twins). An Asian studying in America may receive a remark such as "All Asian students excel". A relative may say, "Everyone in your family is a high-flyer; your dad, your mum, your uncle, etc." Or you get a comment like, "Your elder sister did very well in school." Or if you have a twin brother who excelled in sports, studies and everything (it does not matter if it is a fraternal or identical twin). A child seeing these examples may feel that his/her value and identity are in external achievements, perfection, talents and praise-worthiness. Being in a family or community where moral-religious uprightness is actively encouraged and practised can also, in combination with other factors, instil a strong preoccupation for perfection, high-performance and praise-worthy behaviours from a very young age.

However, therein also develops a dread/fear of "falling short", which can be kept at bay by excelling. Parents with good intentions may encourage good performance and such. But it is also not uncommon for such children to be very self-driven and their parents reminding them that there is no need to excel could fall on deaf ears. Parents also feel that it is right and natural to express joy when such a child succeeds, unintentionally giving more value to external praise-worthiness. But no one would be aware that there is an "inner absence of affirmation"[1]—neither the parents nor the child. With this, same-sex attractions can arise without any shaming, abuse, bullying, nor any kind of family dysfunction or attachment style problems.

A variation of this reason may not pertain to high performance. For example, a parent may be pre-occupied in taking care of a sibling or twin who is always sickly without worrying about the child who is able to take care of himself/herself competently. Such a parent may explain that they should take care of themselves so as to enable Mum/Dad to take care of their sick sibling or twin. And some parents are grateful for this. It is all logical to the competent child, but the same child cannot understand why they sometimes feel resentment. Their competent outer selves distract them from being aware of their need for an inner affirmation.

Another variation is hyper-masculinity. The boy may be extra conscious about how to be masculine. This exaggerated concern may manifest outwardly, such as swaggering, talking tough, enduring punish-ing training and acting out anything "masculine". He may get signs of approval from peers or from family and community, especially if prejudice against homo-sexuals exists. But hyper-masculinity can be driven by an "inner absence of affirmation"[1]. Even if same-sex attractions do not develop, such a person can cause another boy's inferior-masculine complex to worsen, contributing to hyper-masculinity and/or his attractions to the same sex to increase. Hyper-masculinity can also cause aversion in females towards males, contributing to females finding emotional connection only with the same sex and/or misandry in females.

Another surprising yet common enough situation that I have seen is when one or more siblings was "bad or deviant" in the eyes of the parents while the person who eventually develops same-sex attractions is the "good and perfect child". One or both parents may react terribly to the sibling(s) with chiding, tongue-lashing or harsh punishments, and witnessing these can affect the good-perfect child. Such a child is "frozen" in behaving and performing well. Yet, such a child may also see nothing wrong in what his/her parents have done because they have assimilated their parents' ideas of what is right and wrong: "It was all for our own good."

Notes

1. "Inner absence of affirmation" is hard to detect when the person is very talented, capable and high-performing. One sign that it exists is what happens when the person "falls short" or is unable to keep up or perform. There would be a disproportionately large disappointment or over-reaction to compensate, because of the lack of affirmation at the core.

2. None of these happens intentionally. Yet, many parents reading this would have strong feelings of regret and guilt. In conservative-religious communities, even if their children seem fine, well-adjusted and

heterosexual, parents reading this may still feel stricken because same-sex attractions are often not expressed outwardly and can be so hidden (see Chapter 5 for details). This feeling of regret and guilt is natural but can be made worse if parents also have un-affirmed cores. Parents with un-affirmed cores tend to have children with un-affirmed cores, but this does not mean that homosexuality will manifest. On the other extreme, parents with un-affirmed cores can deny, belittle or disparage this information—unless their children's homosexuality explodes into their consciousness. Such parents are also prone to reacting negatively when they discover that their child "is not normal". If supporting homosexuality in society becomes strongly politically correct, such parents are also likely to "give in and support".

3. While any factor from these "groups of reasons" can exist alone, they can also co-exist together. For example, it is not uncommon for a person with good, busy parents and high-performing siblings to also have Anxious-Attachment Style, which developed as an infant when the primary caregivers were too busy to be properly attuned to the infant. And while any combination of these reasons can exist without resulting in homosexuality, their presence will certainly multiply the effects of other factors, increasing the likelihood many times over.

4. A highly recommended book that happens to go much further than this chapter is *Drama of the Gifted Child* by Alice Miller (1997).

Causes and Implications of the Un-Affirmed Core

The implications of what causes this un-affirmed core are incredibly important to contemplate. Taking action may mean going against largely accepted norms of striving for success. However, perhaps it is far more important to consider homosexuality not as a problem to solve, but as an indication of greater problems we have yet to recognise. Here are some examples of situations that are already happening in societies and are likely to increase.

1. Emphasis on good name, high standards and praise-worthiness

Implication: We need to consider carefully the dangers of such emphasis in societies, organisations, and institutions of education, public service and religion. If a society extols good name and high standards without wanting to recognise what in its soul is driving it, whether the source of this desire is good or not, then people with un-affirmed cores will exist with little awareness of all the ramifications and consequences. Education in schools and institutions for our children from the earliest age to the highest levels of education may push hard for these. And people of all religious faiths will not be free of this problem either if they do not recognise the danger of "showing goodness", "showing piety", "showing righteousness" and even "showing humility". When the core is affirmed, there is no need to show. This explains why even praise-worthy upright religious families, with no sign of dysfunction, are not exempt from the possibility of homosexuality. I would even say that religious instruction will lack depth if the difference between "outer value" versus a valued core is not known.

2. Busyness of both parents or primary caregivers, or neglect of finding a good care-giver, thereby affecting the child's attachment style, especially in the early years of life

Implication: We need to reconsider carefully the consequences of calls to have both parents working; of encouraging the business of providing "early child-care centres" in a profit motive environment; and of allowing striving-efforts to get rich as a predominant good. Other factors that may make it necessary for both parents to work should also be carefully considered not only by politicians and leaders of communities but also by couples intending to start a family. If there are no close relatives or persons to take care of the child, arrangements to move the child frequently from one caregiver to another would also increase the risk of affecting the child's attachment style. Last but not least, a primary caregiver not being attuned to a child can easily happen for a multitude of reasons besides busyness, including the caregiver's own unresolved needs and attachment style.

3. Culture or practice of "shaming to drive a person to do better" or "instilling fear in children that they can only be loved and valued if they can behave, perform, be smart, do well, etc."

Implication: Parents and people in authority need to have the courage to question their own unconscious unmet needs and un-affirmed cores. The consequences of not addressing this culture will be increased bullying, denigration, prejudice, ostracisation, injustice, and abuse of power or authority. Communities can help by increasing their ability to educate such parents and people in authority and attend to issues such as unresolved personal psycho-emotional needs.

4. Bullying, denigration, prejudice, ostracisation, injustice, abuse of power or authority

Implication: There is an urgent need to take firm action to stop these in schools and institutions. But it must be strengthened by understanding its causes as mentioned in point 3 above.

Case 8

Tia is the second of two girls. Both girls excel in school. Mum is a housewife and Dad works in an office. Both love and care for their daughters, and are great parents. They all practise their religious faith regularly as a family, as it is an important part of their lives. The girls do well in music and sports. The family celebrates together whenever anyone wins a prize or scores top grades. But Mum knows that Tia is very competitive. Whenever her elder sister succeeds in something, even though outwardly Tia rejoices, Mum knows that inside, Tia feels a strong compulsion to do just as well or even better. There was no need to push Tia or remind her to do her homework. On the contrary, both Mum and Dad often remind Tia that she does not need to excel. Even though Tia acknowledges this, it largely falls on deaf ears. Tia would work doggedly to get the grades and performance standards she wants.

At the age of 12, Tia had her first bout of depression. She was involved in a school team project, and the elder girl in charge was pushing and scolding everyone. "We felt the stress to get things right and done on time." Tia's depression started towards the end of the project, and it lasted for two weeks.

The second bout happened about eight months later. Both she and her elder sister were helping in an event that lasted a few days. They helped in registering, guiding, and giving out brochures. There were lots of people, noise and things to do. Tia felt the stress from the first day, and the depression started on the last day of the event. It lasted for two weeks.

The latest bout of depression was triggered when Tia realised she was attracted to her best friend, also a girl. The thought of the possibility of not being able to do anything about it (homosexuality) sent her spiralling down into depression. She was very determined to get out of it. And she went about it in the same stubbornly unyielding way as she did many other tasks she set her mind to achieve. Her need to show that she is "good" and in control was very strong. But the unconscious feeling of "not being in control" was also too much. The cognitive dissonance (see Chapter 6 for explanation) was strong enough to push her to self-harm—cutting herself—which she tried to conceal. Painful headaches began, and became a daily occurrence.

* * *

When Tia's un-affirmed core was identified as a possible source of her compulsive "drive for excellence", and how it developed was determined, some concrete measures were worked out with her and her parents. When asked when she first felt the need to "perform well", she replied, "Four years old. That's the time when I could see my sister's successes." It must be emphasised that this is through no fault of her parents. Children easily conclude erroneously. And when they take on a self-drive to do well, parents are usually happy. In this case, her parents did notice her strong compulsion and constantly reminded her that she need not excel, but they also did not want to curtail her desire to "do good and do well". When her successes were celebrated or praised, unknown to anyone, her erroneous belief of "if I perform well, then I am valued" was reinforced, and her core remained un-affirmed. In schools, teachers who push their students to excel and highlight students who do well also unwittingly strengthen the problem. Opportunities to affirm the core are most when success is not achieved, or when a child can never be as good as the others. Tia is currently improving, and her daily headaches have disappeared.

I must add that in this case, even though cognitive dissonance was present, it was not reduced by any of the four types of (erroneous) cognitions as described in Chapter 6. Tia brought the problem up to her parents early, and help was sought. If, like in many cases where the child does not dare to bring up the problem, but instead searches the Internet for answers, then it becomes likely that a combination of any of the four (erroneous) cognitions is believed, in order to reduce the dissonance. And this would be held on to strongly for a sense of survival.

People with an un-affirmed core would also exhibit a few traits that are commonly found in people experiencing same-sex attractions. Keep in mind that parents or people in authority with un-affirmed cores will also likely pass it down to the next generation.

a. They are unable to be "lesser" or "disabled" people. For example, a doctor who treats accident patients can be extremely capable and nice. But if the doctor with an un-affirmed core were to suddenly be struck with an accident that makes him/her disabled, that doctor will be unable to accept being helpless. They will over-exert themselves to try to get out of it. Otherwise, they would likely say, "It is better to die." They would likely feel worse if family members exhibit unspoken signs of "being burdened or distressed" due to their own un-affirmed cores.

b. They are hyper-sensitive to any perceived innuendoes that they are "less worthy" or "sick" or "not normal".

c. They will want to be in positions that have statuses (of any kind) that are considered normal, worthy or highly valued.

d. If possible, they will want to be in positions that are able to influence the law to recognise new statuses that would further this need (for being better-valued and for protection from any form of derision or discrimination).

CHAPTER 5

Stages of Awareness

The stages of awareness of one's own attraction to the same sex are an important explanation, especially in conservative-religious communities. The different stages explain the many struggles happening in desperate silence, some below consciousness, almost always hidden. At every transition, there is great internal turmoil for the person experiencing same-sex attractions. This depends on the culture and community in which the person lives and the way he/she comes to understand homosexuality. Not everyone moves automatically from Stage 1 to Stage 3. Some cannot get past Stage 1. For those who do, some choose to stay hidden in Stage 2 in various ways. Comparatively few in conservative-religious communities move on to Stage 3.

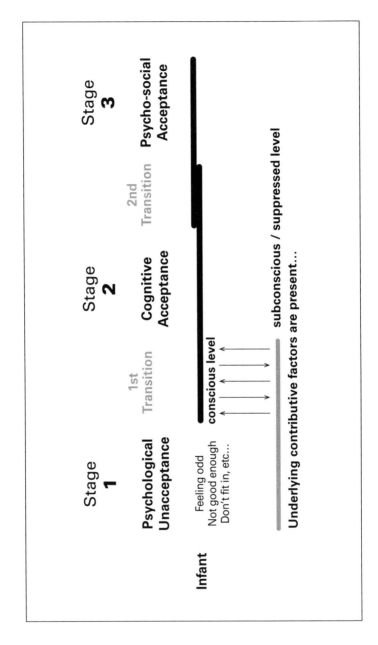

When the factors that increase the possibility of same-sex attractions are present, three stages of homosexuality awareness are possible. (It is important to note that these three stages exist only if there are disturbing feelings that come with experiencing same-sex attractions.)

Stage 1—Before puberty, a child may admire, feel attracted to, or be drawn to someone of the same sex. If factors like being bullied or being disfavoured are present, these feelings may be strong, although not sexualised yet. If a connection between these feelings and homosexuality is made, then dismay, wishing "it will pass away" and "measures to be more normal" may arise, especially if familial, cultural or religious notions against homosexuality exist. During puberty, if sexualisation occurs, there can be great internal dismay. Then Psychological Unacceptance can arise strongly, with active denial/suppression of his/her own same-sex attractions.

In extreme cases, the person remains in Stage 1 throughout life. Such a person can be staunchly against homosexuality. Fear of interacting with gays or lesbians can manifest through psychological projection. However, in most cases, the person in Stage 1 would psychologically avoid facing anyone wanting to talk about homosexuality because they cannot accept such thoughts in their own mind. They would distract themselves with "worthy tasks" or "things to do". This is not difficult because perfectionism, high standards and the fear of being "not-good-enough" are common among them. They may marry heterosexually or enter into religious-celibate life as these are socially acceptable signs of being "normal". The underlying factors that increase the possibility of experiencing same-sex attractions would still have a negative bearing on their relationships even though they have a strong desire to be upright and do everything good. Their spouse may bear the brunt of their perfectionism and fears of "not being good enough". So would those who live with them in a religious community. If they have children, what they do not have is what they cannot provide, and what they value (outer performance) is what they would want their children to have.

Note

Most poignantly, people in Stage 1 do not want to engage in any discussion or education about homosexuality or any form of sexual deviation. The discomfort feels just too close. If they are people with some authority, they may even ban such discussions. More often, they would find passive ways to avoid allowing such talks and education to happen. At best, they may adopt a stand that is politically accepted in the institution they are in and is also safe for themselves.

*   *   *

First Transition: Characterised by internal swings between denial and anxiety. This transition, often during puberty, is further complicated by other problems stemming from the factors that increase the possibility of experiencing same-sex attractions.

Initially, the child may not even be able to say the words "gay" or "lesbian" or "homosexuality". Just the concept itself is so unacceptable. Suicide risk can rise up to nine times the normal rate. This depends on the amount of dissonance felt and the presence of factors such as bullying, denigration, shaming, poor family dynamics, etc. There could be a private bargain with God to "take this feeling away if I promise to (do this and that)…" Such bargains and hope can remain well into the next stage of awareness. In general, the more moral instruction and moral sensitivity the person has, the more there will be internal struggles, anxiety, swings with denial, confusion, fear of being found out, and desperate hope for a cure or miracle.

This first transition need not begin during puberty. Just as a person can remain in Stage 1 throughout life, this transition can occur at any age. The transition may begin when there is an increasing perception that society's attitudes towards homosexuality are more liberal and accepting. This explains why there are men who, despite being married for many years, want to come out "suddenly" to explore or "claim" their identity as homosexual, even elderly men with grandchildren. Also, a person in stable Stage 1 can be triggered into a tumultuous transition when he/she unexpectedly falls deeply in love with someone of the same sex. Strong resistance fuelled by anti-homosexual beliefs can intensify and prolong the struggles in this transition.

*　　*　　*

Stage 2—*Cognitive Acceptance* is reached when the person, through all the struggles described above, finally acknowledges to himself/herself, "I think I'm gay (or lesbian) and looks like it will not go away." The reality of what is felt is now at a sufficient level of consciousness. And with it, the feelings of dismay, moral dissonance, fear, anxiety, etc., all rise more often to consciousness. It can be said that they arise more powerfully than denial and suppression. Yet, the person experiencing homosexuality in Stage 2 may never tell anyone that they experience homosexual feelings. He/she may now wonder alone, "What do I do or be now? How do I live with this? Do I stay in the closet? Can I find someone I can trust enough to know what I have or am? What are the risks? Is there more information I can find? What direction in life is there for people like me? Can I get married and keep this a secret? Or should I join in religious training to become a celibate monk or priest or imam, etc.?" Having a double life, unconsciously or consciously, is common. For some, the contrast between the outer/public life and the inner/private life is small; for others, the contrast is large.

On one end, if the contrast is low and the person is generally able to engage in meaningful work, is generally respected by society and the community, and is by and large able to minimise falling into vices such as pornography, alcohol, addictive behaviours, etc., then the person can stay in Stage 2 for long periods, perhaps for the rest of his/her life. Such a personal journey also fuels the belief that "There is no need to talk about these issues. Everything will be fine."

On the other end, however, if the contrast is large, a feeling of being "inauthentic" or being "never fully understood for who I really am" can arise with increasing dissonance. And this can push the person with these attractions, desires and yearnings into the second transition, which is described on the next page.

Note

If the contrast of the double life is large and the consequences of coming out are huge—for example in a scenario where the person experiencing same-sex attractions is a respectable community or religious leader but has active homosexual fantasies and private acting out, and the social community remains prejudiced and ignorant about homosexuality—a particular kind of psychological dissociation can develop to unconsciously sidestep the feelings of inauthenticity and hypocrisy. This dissociation can keep the two lives diverging where one personality becomes very different from the other in the same person. This increases the risk of scandal that can harm not only the people around when they find out, but also the person with this double life. Both the scandalised people and the person caught out would not be able to "realise suddenly" that it is the same person. The humiliation and shame will be very great. Thus, the impetus to "protect privacy, not allow any probe, ensure proper cover-ups and not expose the problem" will also be very great. This enables double lives, dissociation and hypocrisy to continue. The intensity of scandal risks increases while the leadership and activities of such an institution may be showy and ostentatious, yet hollow and irrelevant at the core. The forces that work through the "fear of losing respect" are comprehensive and powerful.

*   *   *

Second Transition: The next stage of homosexuality awareness is to "come out" and "be accepted and understood for who I really am". In conservative-religious communities where prejudice and misconceptions are high, coming out can be fraught with risks, including losing family, cultural and social ties; facing rejection, derision, condemnation, ostracisation, and maybe even violence. However, besides the feelings of incongruence and being inauthentic, other factors from one's personal history that increase the possibility of same-sex attractions can also continue to assail the person with feelings of "never fitting in", not really being accepted, never really being understood, being isolated and isolating oneself out of fear—and thus the deep loneliness—can push them to find a community that accepts them as they are. This search can go on for many years without anyone noticing, thus prolonging this transition. Carrying out anonymous searches via the Internet exposes the person to a myriad of possibilities. The choices the person makes depends on the amount and quality of moral defences the person has. Institutions as described in the note on page 87 (before Second Transition) will not be able to provide and teach such moral defences.

*   *   *

Stage 3—When a person experiencing same-sex attractions finally finds a group/community that accepts him/her as he/she is, he/she experiences a huge relief. And they can actually feel physically better. This is in contrast with living with the myriads of physiological problems associated with feeling isolated, not accepted, denigrated, looked down upon, etc. Only when the person experiencing same-sex attractions finds social-community acceptance would this physiological contrast be felt. The improved feelings of well-being can be great enough to convince the person to "never go back". This may change much later on when further problems arise from joining the accepting community[1]. But in general, they stay on for a long time.

While it is difficult for conservative-religious communities to provide blind or shallow acceptance, *it is possible* for them to provide fully informed acceptance if they are fully educated. If a conservative-religious community understands the challenges of experiencing same-sex attractions, and is able to provide informed guidance and support for anyone experiencing same-sex attractions or opposite-sex attractions, then these three stages would not apply. Persons with same-sex attractions in such a community would simply be in Stage 3 just as people with opposite-sex attractions simply would be as well. This is possible when communities are more thoroughly educated about the issues behind and around same-sex attractions, just as they should be about heterosexuality or about any minority group. The benefits are not only huge but far-reaching. The more comprehensive and deep the education, the greater the benefits. But the obstacles to bringing the community to this informed level of acceptance can also be huge, as described in the notes under Stages 1 and 2.

Fitting this Understanding into Confounding Cases

Especially in conservative-religious communities, many cases of people coming out as gay or lesbian confound parents, family and friends. There might be comments like, "But he was a nice straight guy. I knew him from when he was young. I just don't understand how he could be gay. Maybe he was brainwashed. Maybe he was sexually molested. Maybe his gay friends influenced him. Maybe… maybe…" A man or woman could be married with children, and then decides to come out as gay/lesbian. However, in all such cases, it is important to check for background factors. Thereafter, the movement from Stage 1 through to Stage 3 could be traced.

The transitions can occur at any age. Social attitudes that increasingly become liberal with media showing images of "gay happiness" can of course influence the movement. There are cases of grandparents coming out as gay, leaving behind spouse, children and grandchildren. The media has a role, but it cannot be solely blamed. It is the background factors that are already there that usually have greater influence. That is why, when they finally do come out, almost all of them say that they have been this way even before what their parents, family and friends may think.

For females, while things can be similar, there are other factors that can make each case more complex. A young woman can truly be heterosexual, marry a man, and after marriage if he turns into a terrible husband who is violent or cheating, it can turn her away from men. And thereafter, her emotional needs could be met only by another woman. Often though, her background history would include factors that predispose her to flip to the other side. Entering a marriage with the belief that it will not be like her parents' bad marriage; a family practice of favouring boys (common in some Asian cultures), witnessing bad patriarchy (which may not be conscious because there is no vocabulary for "patriarchy" in their culture), are just some examples.

Cases where the person is in Stage 1 can be more confounding. The person can openly disagree with homosexuality and not support any LGBT movement. But again, the existence of background factors is important. If the family with whom the person in Stage 1 grew up in is unduly strict; if parental role models are not good; if the person is the only boy among many female siblings; if the person struggles to keep up with the rest of the class or is not valued; if there were many instances when the person was shamed or denigrated—all these are examples of factors that may exist in a person in Stage 1. If violence and injustice are also part of the person's life, then he/she can even manifest his/her frustrations through violence against sexual minorities or anyone identifying as part of the LGBT community. This exists in many countries all over the world.

Movement in the Opposite Direction

In conservative-religious societies, especially in Asia, it is possible for a person to move in the opposite direction, from Stage 3 to Stage 2 or from Stage 2 to Stage 1. For example, when a daughter comes out to the family as a lesbian, the family reacts in such terrible ways that the daughter eventually goes back to living a double life (in Stage 2) where she keeps her homosexual feelings to herself and never mentions it to anyone again. The family becomes fine with that and life goes back to normal while the underlying issues (which in such cases can include unhealthy enmeshment, manipulation and dependencies) are not addressed. Or in another example, where a young man in Stage 2 assimilates and internalises strong anti-gay rhetoric that pushes any thoughts and musing about homosexuality out of mind and consciousness. From a young man cautious and anxious about the attractions he is experiencing, he regresses into Stage 1 and becomes hard in his outlook towards anyone LGBT, I or Q.

Case 9

Mira is a mother of a boy and a girl. She usually feels down and has been on the verge of suicide a number of times. Her husband is well-respected in their country's capital city. He is also involved in various activities in their community. He is a perfectionist. He criticises and emotionally denigrates her for the smallest of mistakes. In their community culture, being seen as upright is very important. Outwardly, their family is regarded as a good and perfect model.

A few years earlier, she saw his text messages, which shocked her. It seemed like he was having an affair. But later, she was even more shocked to learn it was with a man, not a woman. She felt her world had collapsed. She mustered her courage and asked him about it. He went pale in a kind of panic. He apologised and became very nice. But it lasted only for a few weeks. Then he was back to his high-functioning perfectionist self. Whenever Mira brought up the subject, he would belittle her saying, "Ha! You are still ruminating while I've put the problems behind and moved on. It is you who is still stuck in past problems." He resumed criticising and denigrating Mira. Everything went back to "normal".

When asked specific questions about her husband, Mira was able to reveal that he would not speak about his childhood or his father. It was as if he wanted the memories to be erased. She described his mother as terribly overbearing, who fought a lot with her husband and her relatives. Mira's husband is very much against homosexuality and is worried about his children growing up in an increasingly pro-LGBT world. He remains very involved in his religion's activities.

* * *

Unfortunately for Mira, on realising what it takes to make her husband realise what he is doing—and to help him consider the reasons why—she concluded that it would be too much of an upheaval for herself, her family and her community. Her husband's background factors (poor relationship with his father, an overbearing mother, perfectionism, and strong personal prejudice against homosexuality) are some indications that he is likely in Stage 1. He may have fleeting entries into Stage 2 but, thereafter, on realising the consequences, is firmly back in Stage 1. Even though he is far from being gay, the harm and damage he is causing is not at all small. But more importantly, because of a powerful need to be regarded as "upright", he would fight vigorously against any innuendo about him having homosexuality or issues he should be attending to.

So, Mira decided not to continue seeking help. This is very sad because her children were already showing signs of being affected, like perfectionism, moodiness, and declaring they do not want to get married: "Both of you are always fighting, so what is so good about marriage?" As Chapter 4 explains some reasons behind uprightness and perfectionism, what a parent does not have is what they cannot give to their children. And what they value is what they will pass on.

Note

If the accepting community also involves unhealthy matters such as politicking, hypocrisy, betrayal, power struggles, vices, abuse, alcohol, drugs, emotional dependencies, manipulation, enmeshment, emotional violence, etc.—any or all of which any accepting community can have—then problems that arise can cause the person in Stage 3 to search for another accepting community.

CHAPTER 6

Cognitive Dissonance

The work on Cognitive Dissonance by Leon Festinger is worth revisiting for us to understand what a person experiencing same-sex attractions might be going through. Actually, it comes as no surprise that all of us at some point in our lives might experience cognitive dissonance as we face the challenges of life in work, career, relationships, family and religion. However, as we learn more, we find that a person experiencing same-sex attractions struggles for much of their lives without being able to identify the real reasons for their homosexual feelings. Many times they wonder if God or nature made a mistake as they feel themselves rather odd. Throughout their lives, they constantly work at coming to terms with themselves to reduce the cognitive dissonance about their sexual identity.

Definition: Cognitive dissonance is the mental distress or discomfort experienced by a person who simultaneously holds two or more contradictory beliefs, ideas, or values, or when confronted with new information that contradicts existing beliefs, ideas, and values.

An example is when someone thinks: "I have these feelings, but my religion says it's wrong."

Dissonance can be reduced in any of four ways:

1. Change the behaviour or the cognition—*I will not follow my religion any more. They have the teachings wrong.**
2. Justify the behaviour or the cognition, by changing the conflicting cognition—*Homosexuality is in-born, so God must have designed it.**
3. Justify the behaviour or the cognition, by adding new cognitions—*Everyone has the right to love.**
4. Ignore or deny information that conflicts with existing beliefs—*It is not harmful. There is no such thing as causes of homosexuality.**

* These cognitions may be false or half-truths, but they are comforting.

If a person experiencing same-sex attraction also does not want to give up his/her religious beliefs, which remain prejudiced against homosexuality, he/she would continue to have high cognitive dissonance, sometimes adding to other suicide risks.

On the other hand, those who have reduced their cognitive dissonance by accepting *comforting cognitions* will experience the distress again if confronted with new information that contradicts these *comforting cognitions*. They may further entrench themselves in these cognitions.

Important Implication

In conservative-religious communities, a young person experiencing homosexuality who dares not speak about it often searches the Internet for answers. What they find that reduces their dissonance may likely be similar to the example of cognitions given earlier. These cognitions need to be sufficiently entrenched before they can have enough courage to "come out of the closet". Thereafter, it will be very difficult to dislodge these cognitions with any old or new information, because, in the first place, they are needed just to survive.

It is thus imperative that we carry the full information with gentleness, compassion, assurance and patience. Positive regard is best conveyed through their hearts and intuition. Try not to engage them with logic. (See further text in Chapter 8 under "What if my child is gay/lesbian? What if he/she asks if I support his/her sexual activities?".)

Going Further into Activism

Once the dissonance has reduced somewhat, the development of activism (and further on to militancy or extremism) becomes possible. The pathways are many and complex. Here is one pathway model that can be applicable. Four elements need to be present:

1. The person experiencing homosexuality (but may not necessarily be open about it) identifies with and feels for victims of anti-gay prejudice, ignorance, discrimination, violence, etc.
2. He/she views the authorities, community and religious leaders as unjust or apathetic about these matters surrounding homosexuality.
3. He/she feels the threat of loss of meaning or significance. He/she might think, "What if they find out who I really am? How can I live with myself if I do nothing while others like me suffer?"
4. He/she continues to hear anti-gay rhetoric, as well as stories of unjust sufferings, all of which fires up their frustration and drives their resolve to act and do something.

In this present day when the Internet provides many stories of unjust sufferings of people who self-identify as LGBT, communities that remain prejudiced and discriminatory or apathetic and uninterested would actually increase the conditions for a person experiencing same-sex attractions to become an activist (or a silent ally) in support of LGBTQ+ causes.

Activism can also develop among friends and family members of people experiencing homosexuality. This is because suffering can be vicariously felt. Cognitive dissonance can also arise to make them choose to support people with homosexuality—"I've known him/her as a good person for a long time. How can this change suddenly just because he/she reveals his/her true self and religion says he/she is bad?"

Case 10

Min-jun is in his second year of military conscription. He is conscientious and knows that he should be a good role model for his younger brother and sister. Together with their parents, the five of them make up a close-knit family.

When their church organised an annual anti-LGBT day two years ago, the family joined in just like everyone else in church. But Min-jun stayed on the sidelines. Dad and Mum were not too concerned, as they knew their son always wanted to have a rounded, balanced view. So when Min-jun started to raise the fact that gay and lesbian people also have feelings and need protection from militant anti-LGBT people, Dad and Mum were not too worried. On the second annual anti-LGBT day, Min-jun raised more objections to the militant anti-LGBT rhetoric. Still, his parents were not too worried. It was only when his father asked what Min-jun would like to study in university after military service that his answer struck them, "I want to study law. I want to fight for the rights of LGBTQ+ people." Dad probed further wanting to know why. That was when Min-jun revealed that he was gay.

Both Dad and Mum could not fathom how this developed. Suddenly, they felt like they could lose their son. As parents, they wondered what they did wrong. Min-jun insisted that they did not do anything wrong and that homosexuality is in-born. And there is nothing they could have done to prevent or change it. It was as simple as that. His parents remained at a loss. Min-jun could see that. He assured them that no matter what, he would still respect them. And if they insisted that he should see a counsellor, he would comply but only because he respected them, not because he believed it would change anything. So, eventually, they did bring him to see a counsellor.

In the first session, Min-jun revealed that he began to notice his feelings towards other boys at the age of 15. But he suppressed it by concentrating on his studies. He did well in his middle school final exams and went to a good school in the next phase. Once in the new school, he could not suppress the consciousness of his homosexuality. And the dissonance it created drove him to search for answers. He did not think he could ask his parents or his church community. So, he asked some friends who seemed more liberal, and he searched the Internet. There he found many articles and testimonies that convinced him that homosexuality is in-born, and that there is nothing to prevent or change it. Once he was convinced, he began to be irritated by the anti-LGBT rhetoric he was hearing in his community and church. It became worse in the army when he saw the witch hunt within for people experiencing homosexuality. He became sensitive to victims' stories of fear, discrimination, derision, being forced to undergo conversion therapies and prayers for deliverance from homosexuality.

In the second session, Min-jun was asked if he was easily affected whenever it looked like he might not achieve the results he wanted. He said no. But on asking his mother, she said yes. Min-jun was quite a perfection-ist. It became clear that Min-jun would not assimilate any new information to replace the original cognition he received. So, he did not have any more sessions.

*   *   *

However, sessions with his parents continued. They were guided to take these measures to undo the ele-ments that lead to activism. They were asked to: (1) Educate themselves about the existence of other young people experiencing homosexuality but are hiding in fear within communities, why they did not choose it, and of the prejudice, discrimination and injustices they receive. (2) Help educate the community and religious leaders about the matters surrounding homosexuality so that they do not remain unaware, unjust or apathetic. (3) Give meaning and significance to their son's desire to help others who suffer such prejudice and injustice. (4) Join in their son's quest to reduce the divide between unaware conservatives and suffering youths experienc-ing homosexuality.

After six months, they reported that they no longer felt like they were losing Min-jun. While he still desires to help those who suffer in silence, he is much more at ease at home. Work is still in progress.

CHAPTER 7

Understanding Intersex and Gender Dysphoria

Children born with intersex conditions are rare. Some experts say the prevalence at birth can be as high as one in 1,500 births. However, ignorance as well as desire to "not reveal due to shame and fear" can make actual recorded prevalence much lower: around one in 15,000 births in an Asian country with good medical services. The average person on the street knows very little about intersex conditions. This chapter aims not only to give a brief explanation but the lessons that can also be applied for people who experience same-sex attractions.

During the first two months of gestation (pregnancy) the part of the foetus that develops into male or female genitalia is the same for a baby boy or girl. If there are androgens (male hormones), the parts develop into male genitals. If there is an absence of androgens, the parts develop into female genitals. See diagram on the next page.

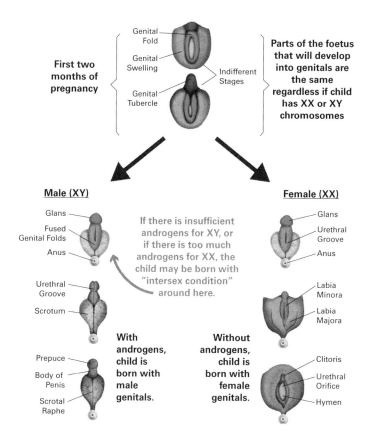

Some kinds of dysfunction can make a boy's body produce too little androgen, or a girl's body produce too much androgens. What can result is a child born with ambiguous genitalia or an "intersex condition". The genitals may look like a small protrusion or tiny penis but with a slit-hole beneath it. In most cases, the child's chromosomes remain XY or XX even though their genitalia may be ambiguous or appear to be closer to the opposite sex.

What Happens When a Child Is Born with an Intersex Condition, and Lessons to Learn

It can be a huge shock for parents. They can be filled with guilt and question themselves, "What did I/we do wrong?" In countries where medical health care includes sufficiently trained paediatricians, the parents may receive explanations, options and suggested guidelines from the doctors. Typically, they learn that their child will need to have some kind of hormone therapy for the rest of his/her life. They could take a year or two to accept and adapt to the situation. Some hormonal therapy may allow the child to have a normal or close to normal physical development. When sufficient guidance is provided, such parents' love for their child is no less, and often more. They will see that their child is totally innocent and lovable. And when they are able to guide their child—like taking medication and being careful to always use private toilet cubicles—then the child will likely grow up with little or no gender identity problems[1].

In fact, many children with intersex conditions grow up and identify themselves as heterosexuals. This is because their condition tends to bring their parents and family closer together, enabling a better family environment where the factors that increase the possibility of same-sex attractions are less likely. This fact also indicates that it takes both "hardware" and "software" to make up a person's sense of gender identity, and that "software" seems to have a significant determining effect. "Software programming" includes good parental role-modelling, healthy father-to-child and mother-to-child relationships, appropriate healthy exposure to people of the same and opposite gender, morally safe and healthy social environments, and much more, all interacting in complex ways.

The Tragedy About Intersex Cases

Despite what the medical field knows about intersex conditions, and the positive outcomes that are possible, the vast majority of parents of people with intersex conditions say: "Please do not tell anyone in my (religious-conservative) community… they would not understand." As such, the individual or family do not receive community understanding or support. On the contrary, they live with a constant worry of being "found out". It is greatly lamentable that some religious people, at the mention of the word "intersex", automatically recoil as if intersex is a sort of conjuring of evil. Indeed, this mentality exists in some third-world communities, where an infant born with intersex condition will be killed. (Search the Internet for "Intersex babies killed at birth".)

As such, it is applaudable that the LGBTQ+ community welcomes people with intersex conditions. But more can easily be done. It is not difficult to bring this knowledge and awareness into conservative-religious communities that enable people with intersex conditions to be accepted and supported in a fully informed way. We should overcome whatever challenges that restrict this education.

Narrative Guide

In the table on the next page, the Narrative Guides that are helpful for people with intersex conditions are also helpful for people experiencing same-sex attractions. The table also helps us understand the proper use of terms. The person is not disordered. It is proper to say "a child with DSD" or "a person experiencing same-sex attractions". It is not proper to say "a DSD person" or "SSA person" or "they are experimenting with SSA" or "we do not condone SSA sort of activities". The right use of words and phraseology in communication is necessary so as not to identify a person with what they are experiencing.

	Reference	Contributory Factors	Narrative Guide
Intersex or **DSD** (Disorders of Sexual Development —a medical term)	**XY**	1. Partial Androgen Insensitivity Syndrome (PAIS) 2. Klinefelter Syndrome 3. Swyer Syndrome (without functional gonads)	"Something did not function properly, preventing you from having a fully male body. **It is not your fault.** You are still very special to us and loved."
	XX	1. Congenital Adrenal Hyperplasia (CAH) 2. Progestin Induced Virilisation 3. Turner Syndrome (45, XO or 45, X karyotype).	"Something did not function properly, making you virilised and more masculine. **It is not your fault.** You are still very special to us and loved."
Same-Sex Attractions	**Physically Male**	1. Bad relationship with father 2. Bullied by other boys 3. Too-close relationship with mother 4. Parents fighting 5. Always feel not good enough… etc.	"Something happened or did not happen during your growing up years. **It is not your fault.** You are still very special to us and loved."
	Physically Female	1. Not close with mother 2. Unable to fit in with other girls 3. Feels "right" being with boys 4. Abused/outraged by males 5. High standards and fit in performance… etc.	"Something happened or did not happen during your growing up years. **It is not your fault.** You are still very special to us and loved."

Important Differences Between Same-Sex Attraction, Gender Dysphoria and Intersex Conditions

It is important to distinguish the differences between a person with same-sex attractions, gender dysphoria and intersex condition. The definition for each has been given in Chapter 1's list of terminology. Grouping these different conditions together makes our thoughts polysemous and leads to confusion and conversational disagreement. The table below shows the differences. (SSA is used to denote cases of people experiencing same-sex attractions.)

Terms	Identical Twin Studies	Bio-Medical Contribution	% Prevalence	Ratio
SSA Gay/Lesbian	11% to 14% ‖	**Low to zero**	5% to 15% † 1.5% *	1 : 20 – 7 1 : 66
Gender Dysphoria	39%	**Medium to Low**	0.7% ‡	1 : 142
Intersex	(none yet)	**High to 100%**	0.006% §	1 : 15,000

* This estimate is half of the 3% in the US.
† Average from 51 batches of trainees and novices from various religious houses in Thailand, Malaysia and the Philippines from 2011 to 2018.
‡ Dr S. Rosenthal, Pediatric Endocrinologist, Director of the Child and Adolescent Gender Center, University of California, San Francisco.
§ Estimate from the Department of Pediatrics, National University of Singapore.
‖ <http://amazinghealth.com/13.06.24-identical-twin-studies-prove-homosexuality-is-not-genetic>.

Intersex conditions are the most heavily influenced by biomedical factors while same-sex attractions are the least. The corresponding "Identical Twin Studies" shows the percentage of the other twin having the same issue if one twin has SSA, gender dysphoria or an intersex condition. SSA has the highest prevalence while intersex has the lowest. Thus, high prevalence is inversely correlated to biomedical contributions.

In terms of "'clarity' in management", intersex is "easiest" because management is predominantly medical, with some counselling-psychology support. Same-sex attractions are "not so easy". It is predominately a psychosocial matter with many factors interacting in complex ways. The information in this book is mainly about understanding people who experience same-sex attractions, to help conservative-religious communities to redefine their attitudes and responses, and what issues surrounding homosexuality need further attention.

The most difficult in "'clarity' in management" is gender dysphoria. Very few hospitals or ministries have an idea about the coordination required between doctors and counsellors (or mental health professionals) medically, psychosocially and spiritually. For example, in Asia, there is a common belief that if a parent dresses a boy in girl's clothes or a girl in boy's clothes, this will cause the child to want to be of the opposite sex. In reality, attention should be on the reasons why the parent dressed the child this way. Often, the parent did not want a girl (or a boy), and the child picked this up. If the child is the same sex as the parent, the child may introject the parent's own sense of "I'm not good enough". Such internal scripts coupled with the child's desperation to be loved and/or not abandoned can affect in complex ways with other factors such as emotional enmeshment to derail the child's internal gender identity. Since human consciousness takes up only 5 per cent of our brain's activity, I would suggest that instead of viewing gender dysphoria as "a boy trapped in a girl's body" or "a girl trapped in a boy's body", we should begin to think of it as "a boy's body trapped in an internal identity of a girl" or "a girl's body trapped in an internal identity of a boy". This might pave the way for better research to help such cases. (There is little mentioned in this book about gender dysphoria because of insufficient experience in helping such cases. However, more text can be found in the last paragraph on page 26, and in the first paragraph on page 44.)

To find out more about the influence of genes on homosexuality, the book *My Genes Made Me Do It!: Homosexuality and the Scientific Evidence* by Neil and Briar Whitehead (2000) is highly recommended. Its fifth edition was published in January 2018. Summarising more than 20 years of research on homosexuality, it draws on more than 10,000 scientific papers and publications from all sides of the debate. This book also tells us about the important role played by the American Psychological Association (APA). The research is orthodox, and objective, undertaken by a New Zealand scientist who has a Ph.D. in Biochemistry, and whose international career spans over 40 years. More information can be found at www.mygenes.co.nz.

Note

1. There are cases where the intersex condition is not detected until later. In such cases, confusion and worry can easily arise, usually around early adolescence. Such cases include late-onset Congenital Adrenal Hyperplasia, where the synthesis of hormones produces too much androgens. A girl may develop normally until this condition arises; her clitoris starts to extend, she may notice the change and become fearfully worried, or other girls may notice and react with derision. Other cases include Complete Androgen Insensitivity Syndrome, where the body cells are completely insensitive to androgens. The child is then born with complete female genitals even though the child has XY chromosomes. The child grows up as a girl until it is noticed that puberty does not occur. But if such cases are brought to the attention of competent doctors with access to endocrinologists, the condition can be explained and medical-hormonal therapy administered. The realisation of the implications of the condition can be distressing both to the child and family. But if attended to competently, the distress can eventually subside.

CHAPTER 8

Answers to Commonly Asked Questions

Do keep in mind that the answers to these questions are for people in conservative-religious communities who ask these questions.

1. Is same-sex attraction in-born?

Even though no gay gene has been found, it certainly feels in-born to those who experience these attractions. That is a phenomenological reality. No child willingly chooses it. There are hundreds of studies trying to find a gay gene. A recent large genetics-based study[1], published in August 2019 in the *Science Journal*, concluded that it was not possible to determine sexual orientation by looking at genes. And numerous identical twin studies show low percentages of the other twin being gay if one twin is (see table on page 110). But psychodynamically, the factors contributing to same-sex attractions are many, complex, of varying depth, and affect mostly at the unconsciousness level (see Chapters 3 and 4 for the factors). A skilled psychodynamic practitioner or counsellor should be able to recognise the factors in a person's life that contribute to the development of same-sex attractions. These factors and their effects can be ongoing.

2. Can same-sex attraction be cured? What can be done?

A cure should not at all be mandated nor intended. In reality, slow progress does more harm when expectations set in desperation are high. However, all cases deserve a good listening by an appropriately trained person if possible. If underlying factors that increase the possibility of same-sex attractions can be identified, measures could be taken to reduce the effects of these factors. Depending on the type, number and intensity of factors involved, some cases can experience a good reduction in same-sex erotic attractions. But some factors cannot be identified (e.g. client cannot remember) or attended to for various reasons (e.g. client is dependent on or unable to detach from a person with personality disorders). Diligence is required to investigate while prudence is required to manage expectations. However, if efforts to "cure" a person are not based on facts but on superstitious/quack beliefs, then more harm will be done.

Another prominent problem is the definition of "cure", or the lack of a definition. Often, it is an unexpressed notion, which can mean different things to different people. Common notions include "being sexually aroused by the opposite sex" and/or preferring "heterosexual pornography". This almost never happens!² I have worked with many good people. Their strong motivation to do what is right and their diligent work have reduced their urges. Some have sublimated their energies into a form of love devoid of lust. Almost all have experienced an increased sense of meaning and well-being. But none of them have experienced the notions mentioned earlier.

Attempting to "cure" a person based on shallow beliefs (quack treatments like shock therapy, aversion therapy, etc.) carries a high risk of causing harm. Trying to "cure" by faith alone also carries a high risk because it is more harmful to raise hope and then fall short. The term "reparative therapy" or any implication that a cure is possible can be highly unacceptable to LGBTQ+ communities. And most "conversion therapies" are done unethically. Many are done by unlicensed and unprofessional practitioners.

However, it is always helpful to remove fear, prejudice, discrimination, and to remain open, welcoming and providing a safe environment for the person. Listening and attending to the underlying factors often helps to reduce the struggles of living with same-sex attractions. Keep in mind that other issues stemming from these factors are almost always at the forefront, not the same-sex attractions.

3. What attitude can we as a community take?

Knowing that having same-sex attractions is not a choice, we can use an analogy of a child born blind or without a limb. We should treat the child with love, dignity, respect, and acknowledge his/her limitations and gifts—everything good people should provide and do for such children.

Continuing with the analogy, if we find more children born like this, one after another, we should ask questions like "Is there something in our environment that's causing this? Pollution? Chemicals? Congenital stressors? Socio-habitual factors?"

1. We cannot neglect the responsibility to search for the cause(s) and find solutions. Suggested areas to look at: pollution of family life; pollution of moral health; pollution of spiritual life and of social values.

2. It is not appropriate to "celebrate" having same-sex attractions, just as it is not appropriate to celebrate having blindness or having physical limitations (see the next point).

3. Each child has the right to ask "Why did God allow me to experience this?" and deserves help to find answers and to find his/her place in society. Instead of celebrating blindly, it is more important to understand the challenges deeply so as to enable a nurturing environment where the child's spirit can grow and shine through the challenges.

4. Collectively, each of us should be part of the extended family that is needed: father figures, mother figures, like brothers, like sisters, and be good role models. It is important to know them well as a family would. Know their inner fears and experiences, and affirm the core of their being. Couples and religious communities who are warm and loving can give affirmation to people experiencing same-sex attractions by including them in their normal activities. Giving them a secure feeling of belonging is extremely life-giving.

4. Who should we reach out to? How can we help?

In conservative and religious communities, there are few people with homosexuality in Stage 3. Instead, there are more people in Stage 2 and Stage 1. With community ignorance* and prejudice, many are deeply hidden; deep in the closet. They would not dare reveal it to their closest friend or seek professional help even if privacy and confidentiality are guaranteed. (*The word "ignorance" in some Western societies carries a negative connotation. For most people in Asia, it means an absence of knowledge. This absence does not detract from a person's dignity or worth even though it is common for Asians to feel shy about their ignorance. However, there are sensitivities to those who look down on their ignorance. This can result in an obstinacy to learn.)

Consequently, if we make the effort to remove our ignorance and prejudices, they may begin to reveal it to their closest friends and families and seek private professional help.

We can even, as a community, reduce the factors that increase the possibility of same-sex attractions in the next generation by addressing social and familial issues that have been neglected, including social morality and moral-development with respect to God's design.

5. What about spouses of people who engage in homosexual activities?

If after marriage, a spouse finds his/her partner is (or has been) engaging in homosexual affairs, it feels much more than a betrayal. Feelings of being used, confused, feeling lost, helplessness, feeling alone, unsure about who to tell, fear of the consequences of telling—can all hit at the same time. Even before finding out, the spouse may already feel something is wrong and may blame him/herself for it. For a wife, her husband's homosexuality often results in challenges to her self-image or womanhood. All these would be compounded if there are children. Often, the (homosexual) partner is not able to provide what he/she has not received as a child, and problems are passed on to the next generation. The finding-out can be so devastating that some spouses consider life not worth living.

Other complications include being on the receiving end of the (homosexual) partner's psychopathologies like perfectionism, suspiciousness of others of the same sex, social isolation, in-law problems due to partner being too close to his/her opposite gender parent, etc. It is thus also important that we do not advocate opposite-sex marriage as a "cure" for someone with same-sex attractions.

6. What if my child is gay/lesbian? What if he/she asks if I support his/her sexual activities?

There are two questions. So firstly, know that those with same-sex attractions often do not have an affirmed core. They may be highly talented high-achievers, which negates any awareness that they have a deep need at their core. And the core is best affirmed in non-verbal ways... received through intuition. So, when they return home, your facial expression, your tone of voice, how you respond in word and action must convey that your child is valued, loved and precious to you. Cook his/her favourite food, pay attention when he/she tells you what happened today, get him/her involved in your activities in ways that affirm his/her value.

As a saying goes: "Love and truth go together. One without the other is destructive." As telling the truth without love is destructive, so is loving without telling the truth. So, before your child subsequently asks you to support his/her sexual activities, find out the truth extensively about same-sex relationships—how much more domestic violence and intimate partner violence (IPV) they have, how much more emotional pain they suffer in cycles over and over again, how much medical and physical dangers they risk, how much more disappointments, betrayals, sense of being taken advantage of, sense of being unchosen, the irony of how paranoia increases as one gets very close, the high rates of depression, sense of being "not good enough", self-harm, thoughts of "the meaninglessness of life", and so forth.

Then tell the truth in love. For example, you could say, "We are worried about you being hurt and of the risk that same-sex relationships carry. But we can only help you make informed decisions. The decision is yours. Even if you choose to do what would make us worried, we respect your decision. Please always remember that if ever someone hurts you and you need a safe place to come back to, you can always come back home."

7. How can we identify those who have homosexuality? Is there a way to know? Wouldn't it be good for parents, pastors, teachers and leaders to know?

An important question to these questions is, "What would you do if you knew who has homosexual feelings?" Would you expose the person? Would you remove him/her from training? Would you mandate him/her to get some kind of "cure", re-orientation or re-education programme? If the person is afraid and resistant, would you mark him/her in some records permanently to "prevent possible future problems"? If there is a strong inclination to do any of these, then there is also a strong unconscious inclination to make matters worse for both the person and for society as a whole, because the underlying issues would still not be addressed.

It is therefore much more important to have the right reasons and motivation—this should be to know what the underlying factors are that cause their deep hidden sufferings. We must reframe our understanding that having same-sex attractions is a symptom of much larger and more important issues in society that have been neglected. This reframing is a proper requisite to wanting to learn more about the factors that increase the likelihood of same-sex attractions.

It is also important to note that persons most interested to learn are the ones who have struggled with homosexuality themselves. Therefore, the only correct motivation for wanting to identify these people is so that we may support them in learning and knowing about the contributing factors. In doing this, they may begin to take action on the issues that give rise to these factors. In doing so, they can also become the best people to help individuals, families, training houses and religious training institutions. They can help to bring everyone to their full potential and to attend to the larger issues in society that contribute to healthy or unhealthy gender-identity and relationship issues.

It is only with this correct motivation and learning that the ability to identify can develop naturally with the right ethics and right responses.

8. Should we have a "zero tolerance" policy to anyone with homosexuality in religious training houses? What is "deep-seated homosexuality" and how can this be diagnosed?

If the "zero tolerance" policy is based on ignorance and fear, then there is a bigger need to get everyone educated to remove the fear—just as learning about the bacteria that causes leprosy can appropriately adjust any "zero tolerance" policy about lepers. However, there may be an even bigger issue to attend to if there is reluctance and resistance to being educated. (See notes in Chapter 5 under Stage 1 and Stage 2, and in Chapter 9 on "Why people in religious institutions are reluctant to talk about homosexuality and how the root of scandals grow".)

It is erroneous to have a notion that "deep-seated homosexuality" can be diagnosed like some medical condition. I would assume that the danger implied by the term "deep-seated homosexuality" pertains to gay activism in support of gay people who suffer inappropriate responses and ignorance. This danger hidden in religious training houses would indeed pose a problem (especially if the word "gay" is not recognised as a polysemy). However, this danger is also akin to racial-religious militancy or radicalisation, which are also fuelled by inappropriate responses and ignorance. LGBT activism can also exist among straight people, who can be more militant than their LGBT counterparts. Hence, this danger can still exist even if everyone experiencing homosexuality is identified and removed.

A person with same-sex attractions who wants to live a virtuous life; who wants to know why he/she is experiencing this; and who wants to know of ways to reduce his/her homosexual struggles, should not have to contend with "zero tolerance" policies or suspicions of "deep-seated homosexuality". Such a person should instead be met with readiness to help in these endeavours. At the same time, just as all institutions and religious leaders must understand the underlying causes of racial-religious militancy and radicalisation, so too must they understand the underlying causes of LGBT activism and militancy. They should then strive to educate everyone.

9. Are there any "success stories" of deliverance from homosexuality? Or will homosexuality always be a "thorn in the flesh until death"?

Firstly, what is your definition of "success"? Does it mean being "cured"? (Please refer to the answer to the earlier question, "Can same-sex attraction be cured?".)

Before going any further, it is important to know that there is a difference between "pure love" and "lustful love". There are studies that show these two use different parts of the brain[3].

A boy's masculinity (or a girl's femininity) can and should be affirmed in ways that are virtuous and pure.

What is most helpful is pure love from people of the same sex that guides and affirms. People who experience same-sex attractions need this kind of love more than anyone else. This includes attending to the unresolved underlying factors. Just as it took many years for these factors to take its effect, it can take many years to reduce the negative effects. However, not all factors can be identified for various reasons. If the factor is distressing or traumatic, the mind may not remember in an effort to not re-live the distress and trauma. A factor like a parent with personality disorders cannot be easily removed. There can be difficulties in wanting to know new information due to cognitive dissonance (please refer to Chapter 6). Nonetheless, progress can be made to enable the person to feel supported and affirmed. They can then find it easier to disregard sexual ways to act out their masculinity or femininity.

However, if they feel neglected, slighted, or feel that their real selves cannot be accepted, or have a constant fear of denigration if they do not live up to expectations, then their vulnerability to temptations will increase and their homosexual feelings can easily be re-ignited. The concept to help keep temptations at bay with love and support is universal and must be applied for both people who have opposite-sex attractions and people who have same-sex attractions. Importantly, it should start from the very beginning of a child's life, not when the fear of homosexuality or sexual promiscuity arises. Thus, the reply to the questions above is not to think about "success" or "cure", but to be informed and to respond wisely.

10. Now that more countries and jurisdictions have banned or are working to ban conversion therapy, what do you think?

Any attempt to "cure" or convert a homosexual that is not based on any sound (psychological) science is highly likely to cause more distress, disappointment, pain and harm. Methods like "aversion therapy" can increase distress as it can include applying something unpleasant—such as an electric shock, beatings, bitter tastes or ant-bites—every time the person with SSA has homosexual feelings. Raising false hopes through "sure-to-work" medicines and performance-rituals are also harmful. Expectations from big groups are particularly harmful because when there is no improvement, the sheer amount of disappointment directed at the person can be unbearable. This is on top of suggestions like "you didn't try hard enough, you didn't do enough of (this and that)" or innuendos of "maybe you had bad/impure thoughts". Thus, in big groups, there can also be pressure to "fake a cure or improvement". This only increases the feelings of incongruence and hypocrisy.

However, if professional ability to identify the underlying factors that contribute to same-sex attractions is available, then doing so to reduce the negative consequences of these factors is highly recommended. The benefits include reducing suicide risk, loneliness, obsessive-compulsive behaviours, stress, perfectionism, need for affect-relief and addictive behaviours, better relationship management and a better sense of affirmation at the core. However, free choice must always be respected. If a person experiencing homosexuality is made aware that this work to reduce the negative consequences would carry the possibility of reducing attractions to the same sex, and therefore the person does not want the work, then his/her wish must be respected.

In short, "gay conversion therapy" of unsound precepts that seeks a "cure" can be banned, as long as the definition of it is accurate, not sweeping nor nebulous. However, sound therapeutic assistance that is able to identify and attend helpfully to the underlying factors that contribute to same-sex attractions and the associated problems should not be lumped together with the above and banned. We must not conflate the two and ban them all.

Notes

1. Findings of a study on the genetic basis of sexuality were published in August 2019 in the *Science Journal*. It is the largest study to date, based on the genomes of nearly half a million people. The study confirms the suspicions of many scientists: while sexual preferences have a genetic component, no single gene has a large effect on sexual behaviours. They found that genetics could explain 8–25% of the variation in sexual behaviour. This implies that the rest of the 75–92% are attributed to other factors such as the environment, society, culture, attitudes, etc.

"The researchers found five single points in the genome that seemed to be common among people who had had at least one same-sex experience... but taken together, these five markers explained less than 1 percent of the differences in sexual activity among people in the study." There are many other genes that contribute. But each of them accounts for an insignificant amount of contribution. "There is no 'gay gene'," says lead study author Andrea Ganna, a geneticist at the Broad Institute of MIT and Harvard in Cambridge, Massachusetts. "This is a solid study," says Melinda Mills, a sociologist at the University of Oxford, UK, who studies the genetic basis of reproductive behaviours. "It's the end of the 'gay gene,'" says Eric Vilain, a geneticist in the Children's National Health System in Washington, DC.

As results of such a topic are prone to misinterpretation, the researchers worked with LGBTQ advocacy groups and science-communication specialists to come up with ways to present their research findings to the public. The efforts included a website that presents the results and their limitations using sensitive, jargon-free language. Even then, misrepresentation of this research, via omitting or cherry-picking parts of the study, still occurs. One example headline in a newspaper: "Many Genes Influence Same-Sex Sexuality, Not a Single 'Gay Gene'."

2. There are rare cases of people who experience same-sex attractions and who also have borderline personality disorder. They can swing from homosexual to heterosexual pornography. However, in such cases, the borderline personality disorder itself causes far more upheavals in the person's life than the struggles with experiencing same-sex attractions. These can be in addition to the negative effects of other factors that increase the possibility of same-sex attractions.

3. From a study report, "Selective Decision-Making Deficit in Love Following Damage to the Anterior Insula", in the journal *Current Trends in Neurology* 7, (2013): 15–19.

CHAPTER 9

Social Dimensions Surrounding Homosexuality

Impact of Social Deviance

In any area where social immorality can increase little by little—when phrases like "it is normal nowadays" is used with little thought; when girls and women generally feel "there are no good boys or men" and feel they have to fend for themselves; when selfish pleasures, advantageous deceit, disguised ruthlessness, ignorance of bad patriarchy, and when having no fear or knowledge of moral defilement, ignorance of the benefits of chastity dominate society—then children who are morally sensitive will be impacted in many ways, including experiencing the factors that increases the possibility of same-sex attractions.

It is not an irony that people with same-sex attractions are often gifted, talented and desire what is good and right in everything they do. (And this is also the reason why religious institutions also have high percentages of people with same-sex attractions.) They have the potential to be the best people to help society out of social problems. When given the full knowledge, help and support, people who have struggled with homosexuality are highly motivated to reach out to help. Not only to people struggling with homosexuality but also to help the many problems associated with it, such as loneliness, bullying, feeling not-good-enough, not feeling valued, feeling fake, relationship difficulties, suffering abuses, witnessing immorality, witnessing impunity, injustice, and worst of all, a constant fear of being hurt or being disliked in self-defeating and exhausting ways. If only the people around them also knew and assisted them, then this help can be expanded greatly.

In contrast to this great potential is the irony that many leaders in conservative-religious communities and institutions do not want to know or deal with the issues that give rise to people experiencing same-sex attractions. Seeing fewer men than women involved in social, community or religious services is a sign that they are not tackling deep important strategic issues that affect society. And so, many good people struggling with same-sex attractions continue to remain hidden within conservative-religious communities.

Reaching People with Homosexuality Hidden in Communities

Sometimes you may know that there are people within our communities who are probably experiencing homosexuality, but they are too afraid to speak about it. They would not seek help no matter how much privacy and confidentiality is assured, and you know they are probably struggling silently underneath. How can we reach them?

Keep in mind that in such cases there are two levels:

1. The personal level—which can be attended to privately and confidentially.
2. The systems level—which pertains to the people around the person: the religious and cultural communities, the workplace, the state and government. Parents and family may straddle between these two levels.

Often, to reach the individual, we have to educate the important people at the systems level first. This can be done by giving educational talks to the community. Some topics that can be integrated include "parenting" or "useful psycho-developmental information for raising children". It is possible to also give a talk directly about "understanding homosexuality". The purpose of these talks should be to remove misconceptions, prejudice, discrimination, and to increase understanding, compassion and readiness to help.

Only when an individual experiencing same-sex attractions sees that the attitudes of the people around him/her have changed and are less prejudiced would that individual dare to ask privately to speak in confidence about their struggles. Oftentimes, we have to create an opportunity for them to speak privately without anyone else knowing of it. If this is difficult in hostels, seminaries and certain groups, then a programme that requires everyone to have a one-to-one session may be feasible.

Why People in Religious Institutions are Reluctant to Talk About Homosexuality and How the Roots of Scandals Grow

In some societies, remaining single and being unmarried raises too many uncomfortable questions from family, relatives and friends. The pressure to be married increases if people with same-sex attractions also frequently seem to be so morally upright, so clean, so talented, so high-performing, and thus more suitable to marry and become a good spouse. Hence, entering religious life that requires celibacy would reduce this pressure.

However, if they enter a religious institution that has strong views against homosexuality to the point that it cannot even be discussed civilly, then only those who are in

Stage 1 (psychologically unable to accept) would join. They will perpetuate the problem by having strong views against homosexuality and may even have an outward anti-homosexual stance (through psychological projection). At best, they will not allow any discussion about homosexuality. This is the reason why it has been, and continues to be, very difficult, if not impossible, to educate them. They will say things like, "The Holy Book is very clear. Homosexuality is a sin. There is nothing else I need to know." They will refuse any activity that educates their faith members about homosexuality because they have deep fears below their consciousness that they will be found out. They will not like anyone to "dig" around. They will not approve of any research or surveys. (Also see Chapter 5, Stage 1 notes.)

As people experiencing same-sex attractions are often talented and high-performing, not just a few rise up in their religious institutional hierarchy. They are often the best teachers, and the best speakers, and are also artistically, musically and liturgically talented. Most importantly, they often possess all the qualities that make them seem like the best people to train the next cohort of religious practitioners.

But if the underlying factors that increase the possibility of same-sex attractions have not been identified and attended to, they will also exhibit many problems associated with people experiencing same-sex attractions—highly driven for perfection and a show of goodness, and even a show of perfect humility. They are often intolerant of imperfection in themselves or in others. They can have hypersensitivity, favouritism, jealousy, and generally high propensities for depression, agoraphobia, mood swings, etc. They will hate each other while everyone outside thinks highly of them. And they will not be able to reveal this, just like people in the gay/lesbian community cannot reveal their higher rates of domestic violence.

Therein lies the danger, which increases the risk of sexual indiscretions in religious communities, but more often than not results in relational hurts and pain that are equally as bad as those experienced among non-religious same-sex relationships.

Some people with same-sex attractions in Stage 2 might consider entering religious life. The lure of being a respected person of religion is strong on account of the un-affirmed core that they have. And if the social culture regards talking about homosexuality as taboo, then they may make the decision to enter into religious life. But once in, if transgressions by other religious are overlooked, then giving in to temptations that increase the risk of scandals will grow. How much it grows corresponds to how much the social culture allows a person in authority to "sort his/her own problems alone". If society places a high level of importance on respecting religious people, then the risk of having scandals can grow to enormous proportions. (See important information in Chapter 5, Stage 2 notes.)

But some time later, someone will find out. Typically, the people who find out are from their own ranks. The consequence is that the faith and sense of integrity of these people are affected, and are sometimes damaged beyond repair. Not uncommonly, a religious trainee will have little option other than to stay in religious training despite witnessing or experiencing moral abuse. This can be due to a variety of reasons, including poverty at home, a dysfunctional family, expectations of the family and relatives, and a lack of having other opportunities. These can be combined with a lack of self-esteem that desires the respect that can be obtained if the religious trainee can somehow "adapt" to complete training and be ordained in a religious order. To withstand witnessing or experiencing these moral abuses, what often happens is a psychological introjection where the values of the abuser become the values of the victim or witness. Thereafter, the moral abuses do not disturb their conscience much. This is how terrible ills like pederasty can develop within a religious system and continue to exist for decades. A kind of automatic "turn-a-blind-eye" can also develop so that, even though there is no involvement in the moral abuses, there is also no response or reaction to stop the moral abuses.

Will Scandals in Religious Institutions Continue?

Scandals will most certainly continue to be uncovered. There are plenty of abuses going on in Asia and many Third World countries that continue to be suppressed and hidden. Cultures that emphasise respect for elders and religious authorities, combined with social ills and bad role models, will continue to draw morally sensitive people struggling with same-sex attractions into such institutions while very little is done to address their unresolved underlying needs.

For sure, not every religious person is an abuser. And many religious trainees do have motivations to do what they can to remove bad habits, temptations, urges to vices, etc. However, out of fear and shame, some try to do so on their own without wanting any help from the outside. If the institution values "good name" and the preservation of "getting respect" over what needs to be done, then much of these efforts get neglected and risks increase. A kind of clericalism that restricts the ability and humility to learn will also add to this buildup.

A sign that the institution is in danger is when nobody in it wants to be the trainer of their religious institute. Some will be appointed anyway, and they take it up with unspoken reluctance. It is a sign that their own religious training contains terrible experiences, which can include being bullied by seniors, witnessing seniors playing cat-and-mouse games to get whatever they want, enduring meaningless routines, learning to "turn a blind eye" to survive, etc. The religious training has little other value except endurance to obtain the rewards of being ordained—to get unquestioned respect, being treated well, living a privileged life, etc. In reality, many cannot withstand such a terrible life during training and thus leave before ordination.

In many Asian communities, victims of abuse are far less likely to speak out. I am not sure if this will change in the future. But as of today, a common sign of the consequences of these abuses is a drop in faith practice. In victims and those who know about the abuses, there is a dislike of anything related to the religion of the abuser. This dislike cannot be spoken of. But it can fester to very high levels of resentment, which results in a disappearance of people from faith practice.

Case 11

This case story spans over several years. The followers of John's religion in his country view psychiatry, psychology and counselling with stigma. They cannot distinguish between them, and most people avoid these services. But religious leaders are still much respected.

When John completed his high school education in a religious hostel, he applied to enter the religious novice training whose head was one of the few religious who believed in using counselling-psychological services. During the counselling interview, John was pleasant and obliging. His father left the family when John was an infant. His mother left him and his brother in the care of an aunt. John spoke well of his aunt but nothing about her husband. John did not like him. While John took the religious path, his brother joined gangs and was into glue-sniffing and drug abuse.

About 50 minutes into the interview, John's demeanor changed. He revealed parts of himself he never told anyone before. In the first two years of elementary school, he was sodomised by older village boys. He felt "dirty" and that "something was wrong" with him ever since. He avoided "bad boys", which in his part of the country can be most boys. When homosexual feelings developed in his teens, he tried to have girlfriends. The first dumped him after three months, the second after one month. He tried very hard with the third, but when she dumped him after a year, his emotional distress increased and became visible. Soon, sexual predators sniffed him out and seduced him. He felt worse because, "I allowed them, but I can't help it." When asked if he could reveal who the predators were, he replied, "Initially, a few strangers. But now, a junior religious student."

John did not pass the entrance test, so he had to return to the religious hostel. He was taught how to protect himself before returning. The head of the novice training was informed about this case. But he had no jurisdiction over the religious hostel as it was in a different state. Attempts were made to enter that religious hostel to address the situation, but the head of that religious hostel did not allow it because he was one of many religious who did not like any counselling services. For one year thereafter, John did not reply to any phone calls or text messages from the counsellor, because he feared this head would find out.

The following year, John applied to enter the noviatiate again. This time he passed, and he could receive counselling. The factors that contributed to him experiencing same-sex attractions were identified, and measures to mitigate them and self-safety boundaries were worked out. He was diligent in these. When he received acknowledgment and support for these efforts from his head, he flourished. He turned into a highly motivated and lively young man.

Then he proceeded to the next level of religious training, where there, again, were many religious who viewed counselling-psychology negatively. While John remained grateful to the counsellor who helped him, he has presently once again stopped replying to any phone calls or text messages from the counsellor. Increasingly, he wants to forget that he ever had a case. He currently shows signs of retreating into himself while he continues his religious studies towards ordination.

* * *

Over many generations, there have been many religious people like John. And there are many other religious people who are silent witnesses. If maintaining the respect of the people is given greater importance, then avoiding "help to attend to deep issues" becomes institutionalised in unspoken and unwritten ways. This also results in a severe lack of will to exercise jurisdiction to address problems.

* * *

The junior religious student-predator was confronted. He was told that he could not proceed unless he admitted to all he had done and received appropriate attention. He agreed to write a confession, but ran off without doing so. He went to another state, into another religious training house, and is now working towards ordination, after which he will be deployed to run schools.

CHAPTER 10

Conclusion

As can be seen in this book, there are many factors that can contribute to homosexuality. As much of these happen below consciousness, the person who experiences same-sex attractions does not choose to have it. On top of that, social prejudice, fears, ignorance, lack of awareness of psychological concepts and insufficient vocabulary, make the understanding of homosexuality difficult and prone to be incomplete and lopsided.

This book does have its limitations. However, I also hope this book will spur researchers to try to measure:

1. The prevalence of each factor described in this book
2. The profile of the prevalence of factors for each culture, religion, country, ethnic group, etc.
3. The prevalence of people in Stage 1, 2 or 3 in each culture, religion, country, ethnic group, age group, etc.

While the challenges to do such research can be formidable, there will at least be knowledge of what to look for.

Regardless of these limitations, I hope this book will be helpful to many people who desire to know how to help those who are impacted by homosexuality directly or indirectly in an understanding and compassionate way. This would be better than feeling conflicted.

For you, the reader, I hope this book has, at least, assisted you in understanding and getting a wider, bigger and more in-depth picture about homosexuality. I hope you can also now see how homosexuality is actually a symptom of far greater problems that impact family life, future generations and society. Examples of such problems are:

- Insufficient outreach to attend to all teenagers. This includes educating and preparing them to be good responsible husbands and fathers, wives and mothers—which should include a compassionate look into their past histories and helping them to identify unresolved psycho-emotional needs that could affect the next generation.
- Insufficient moral-defence education for all children that can last through the next generation of parenthood and families.
- Insufficient efforts to understand the roots of bullying by children and by adults so that bullying can be better tackled (see points 3 and 4 on page 76).
- Insufficient awareness of the importance of teaching both children and adults to be humble, generous and

inclusive to everyone, especially those who need the community to be their extended family.

- Lacking serious attention, understanding and action to tackle the root causes of violence, abuse, harassment, suppression and the devaluing of women—or the emasculation of men—especially those who are weak, have less power, and have less voice.

- Not being aware of bad patriarchy in our family, culture and social systems that puts women at a disadvantage, and of the importance of raising good men to respond to injustices.

- Being distracted from all the above due to pre-occupations and giving undue priority to getting rich and showing "good-face" individually, as a community and as a society.

- Not knowing the difference between outer praise-worthiness and inner worth (see Chapter 4).

On the other hand, being aware of the factors that increase the likelihood of same-sex attractions can bring about many benefits. Areas of benefit that can develop include the removal of misunderstanding, prejudice and discrimination, and raising the need for "gender-development-awareness guidance and counselling". Leaders, elders, counsellors, and other professionals will be able to detect risks and dangers in families, in society, culture and education (that sometimes contribute to terrible hidden suffering that individuals with homosexuality go through without choice). They would then be better informed to help shape the law and government in ways that can help the wide spectrum of issues in an inclusive way.

Importantly, I hope you can see why many in religious life were impacted by the many problems in society because of their moral sensitivity, but also remain deeply hidden out of fear, and so unknowingly subvert themselves from being the best people to attend to society's big issues. This lack of understanding of the factors surrounding homosexuality, combined with a blindness fuelled by the "desire to preserve respect" can result not only in neglect but in the development of serious institutional problems that allow terrible abuses to exist in hidden ways for decades. But I believe everyone can be shaken awake to understand, support and bring them to their full potential. For the sake of humanity, we all should.

In my next book, I will write about some things that can be done by individuals, families, communities and societies to affirm the core. May God give you all that you need to respond in Truth and Love with Courage.

Guide to What Chapters to Read

- What is this gay or LGBT or "coming out" all about? —Chapter 1
- What are the factors that contribute to the development of same-sex attractions?—Chapters 2, 3 and 4
- Are there any cases where homosexuality develops with no abuse or family dysfunction?—Chapter 4
- Why are people with homosexuality often so talented?—Chapter 4
- Why did it take so long for him/her to tell me? —Chapter 5
- Why are suicide rates among homosexuals higher than normal?—Chapters 3 and 6, and the case stories within
- What is "intersex" and "gender dysphoria"? —Chapter 7
- Are there any social trends and factors that contribute to homosexuality?—Chapter 9
- Why do my religious leaders not want to talk about homosexuality?—Chapters 5 and 9
- More questions and answers—Chapter 8

Glossary

clericalism: undue importance given to institutional aspects and hierarchy of an organised religion, often to the exclusion of views of non-elites and non-members. This phenomenon can also exist in purely secular guilds.

congenital: having a particular trait from birth.

disaffiliation: the act of ceasing to be associated with something.

effeminism: characterised by or possessing qualities traditionally attributed to women.

gender: the state of being male or female, typically used with reference to social and cultural definition and differences rather than biological ones. (See Chapter 1, page 4 for this term as well as "Gender Dysphoria" for contextual details.)

grimace: contort the face to indicate a certain mental or emotional state.

homophobic: having or showing a dislike of homosexual people.

individuate: distinguish from others of the same kind.

intra-psychic: being or occurring within the mind or personality.

misandry: dislike of or contempt for men.

neuroticism: a personality trait characterised by instability, anxiety, aggression, etc.

patriarchy: a system of society in which men hold the power and women are mostly excluded from it.

phenomenological: of or relating to the study of the development of human consciousness and self-awareness as a preface to or a part of philosophy.

physicalities: the physical features of someone, or an intense focus on the physical body or the needs of the body.

polysemous: having multiple meanings.

polysemy: a word with many different meanings. (See Chapter 1 for contextual details.)

psychodynamic: relating to the study of interacting motives and emotions.

sex: either male or female into which humans and many other living creatures are generally divided on the basis of their reproductive function. (See Chapter 1 for this term as well as "Intersex" for contextual details.)

visceral: relating to deep inward feelings rather than to the intellect.

Bibliography

Amazing Health. "Identical Twin Studies Prove Homosexuality is Not Genetic." *Amazing Discoveries*, n.d. <http://amazinghealth.com/13.06.24-identical-twin-studies-prove-homosexuality-is-not-genetic> (accessed 30 October 2019).

Bagemihl, Bruce, and Megahan, John. *Animal Homosexuality and Natural Diversity*. New York: St. Martin's Press, 2000.

Bass, Ellen, and Davis, Laura. *The Courage to Heal*. New York: HarperCollins Publishers, 1988.

Bowlby, John. *Attachment and Loss*. 2nd ed. New York: Basic Books, 1983.

Bowlby, John. *Maternal Care and Mental Health*. 2nd ed. Northvale, New Jersey: Jason Aronson, 1995.

Festinger, Leon. *A Theory of Cognitive Dissonance*. Stanford, California: Stanford University Press, 2009.

Hor, Joanna, Ng Zhi-Wen, Bernice Tan, Tan Soo-Inn, Ronald Wong, and Raphael Zhang. *Walking With Same-Sex Attracted Friends*. Singapore: Graceworks, 2018.

Lew, Mike. *Victims No Longer*. 2nd ed. New York: Quill, 2004.

Matheson, David. "What Causes Male Homosexuality." *Genderwholeness*, September 2013 and February 2016 <http://genderwholeness.com/main-cgw-page/under-standing/what-causes-male-homosexuality/> (accessed 30 October 2019).

Miller, Alice. *Drama of the Gifted Child*. New York: Basic Books, 1997.

Truscott, Gordon. *Inside Homosexuality*. Singapore: Armour Publishing, 2011.

Vasey, Paul. *Homosexual Behavior in Animals: An Evolutionary Perspectiv*e. Cambridge, United Kingdom: Cambridge University Press, 2006.

Whitehead, Neil, and Briar Whitehead. *My Genes Made Me Do It! Homosexuality and the Scientific Evidence*. 5th ed. Belmont, New Zealand: Whitehead Associates, 2018.

Wong, Melvin. *Raising Gender-Confident Kids*. 2nd ed. Singapore: Armour Publishing, 2008.